At noon, Fear is nowhere to be found
As shadows stretch,
danger finds a place to hide
In night's darkness. Fear grips us tightly
Faith loosens the grip to set us free

---Ruby Sue Tootser

Hit'em
Before They Hit You

Kelvin Waites

Pp
Prose Press

Hit'em Before They Hit You
Copyright © 2014
Kelvin Waites

All rights reserved. This publication may not be reproduced, stored in a retrieval system, or transmitted in any form recording, mechanical, electronic, or photocopy without written permission of the publisher. The only exception is brief quotations used in book reviews.

Comments: contact@kelvinwaites.com
or visit the author's www.kelvinwaites.com

Find the author on Facebook at
www.facebook.com/KwaitesAuthor?ref=hl
or follow him on Twitter at
twitter.com/WaitesKelvin

ISBN: 978-1-941069-07-3

Published by Prose Press
Pawleys Island, South Carolina
www.ProsePress.biz
prosencons@live.com

Acknowledgments

I would like to first and foremost thank my father, the late Isaac Waites, Sr., for planting a seed in me that is still growing today. He was a master at motivating and inspiring not so much with his words, but with his actions. If it was not for Isaac Waites, Sr., I would not be able to write this book, or be the person I am today. He truly left his fingerprints on the world and a legacy that has no sign of fading away any time soon.

I would also like to thank my mother, Frances Waites, for always reminding me of what my dad stood for. She often reminds me that my father would always tell us to "reach for the sky, because the sky is the limit," even when my brothers and I were not old enough to understand what he meant. I thank Frances Waites for always praying for me and encouraging me to keep pushing forward.

I thank my brothers Isaac Waites, Jr. and Terrance Waites for following through and being the men that our father raised us to be. I appreciate the two of you more than you will ever know. Our father is definitely smiling down on us from heaven.

I would like to thank all of my friends who I have met over the course of the years who have helped me along the way by lending a helping hand, inspiring me, or just by giving me words of encouragement. I also would like to thank the negative people in my life who tried to tear me down, or doubted that I had what it took to be successful. I do not take the negative influences personal because we all should use every experience in our tool boxes to become better people.

Finally, I would like to thank my wife Chelice Waites, my daughter Jasmin Waites, and my son Kelvin A. Waites, Jr. for standing by my side and not letting me settle with being just ordinary. Instead you supported me and pushed me to strive to be extraordinary. I could not have done this without you. Thank you, Jasmin and KJ, for being the type of people your grandfather would be proud of.

Preface

"Hit'em Before They Hit You." You are probably thinking, "what a title." I assure you that it is not a typo and I chose this title because the phrase really means something to me. "Hit'em before they hit you" is what my father told me a long time ago. My father was Isaac Waites, Sr. and despite him only having a sixth-grade education and limited resources, he was the smartest person I have ever known. He grew up in a rural part of Charleston, South Carolina, called Johns Island during the 1940s. Isaac Waites, Sr. was a loving husband and father who didn't just tell his three sons how to be men, but showed them.

Regardless of what race, nationality, age, or gender you are, this book has a message for you. It contains motivational stories and passages of courage, sacrifice, and pure determination. This book is about leadership and how leaders have the power to impact and influence the people they are called on to lead, as well as everyone else around them. It is also about the courage necessary to press on even when you cannot clearly see your way and meeting new challenges head on. Sacrificing your own comfort to put the well-being of others first is what you will read about in this book. "Hit'em Before They Hit You" is about having the will to accomplish your goals while possessing a quiet confidence that demands respect. You will be inspired, you will be motivated, you will be given hope; this book may even set you on fire.

1
Charity Begins at Home

1 Timothy 5:8 But if any provide not for his own, and specially for those of his own house, he hath denied the faith, and is worse than an infidel.

My father, the late Isaac Waites, Sr., was born on Johns Island, which is located in the rural part of Charleston, South Carolina, on July 20, 1939. His parents were the late Wilhelmenia McCray and the late James "Doc" Mitchell, both of Johns Island, South Carolina. Though both of his parents were living he was raised by his aunt, the late Julie Chisholm, who he called Ma or Grandma. He was the first born of his mother, and ended up being the oldest of eight children birthed by my grandmother. My father, his brother Paul, and his sister Delores grew up in South Carolina while Stevie, Richard, Phillip, Julius, and Elizabeth were all raised in New York. Isaac was a normal kid who liked to play outside all day and do regular kid stuff. He got his early childhood education at St. James Church and St. Matthew A.M.E. church, both of which are located on Johns Island. He was not very athletic at all and really couldn't play any sport at a level that would make him competitive with other kids his age. He was a handsome young African-American man with fair-colored skin. He was shorter than average and was on the husky side, but was very studious and well kept.

From what my father told me, his father lived right down the street from where he grew up and he was perfectly aware of who he was. I do know that my father had three step-brothers and three step-sisters. The only one of my father's step-brothers or sisters who I ever really had contact with was my Aunt Carrie. My Aunt Carrie and my dad looked so much alike that it was not hard for me to believe that "Doc" was their father. She was a short lady who was about five feet and two inches tall. She had the same complexion and smooth skin as my dad. My Aunt Carrie was very soft spoken, a very elegant lady, and was always extremely nice to me whenever I saw her; which wasn't very often.

From my perspective and everything that I know about my dad's father, James "Doc" Mitchell lived down the street from my father because he had another entire family that he lived with. This had to be painful for my father to see, and I understand how resentment built up in him over the years. When my father was young, his mom moved away to New York City. No one ever said this, but I truly believe that my grandmother moved up north to avoid the pain of watching my grandfather live with and raise an entirely different family right under her nose. My father never talked much about the living arrangements, but I can only imagine that he would have had serious questions or issues with the fact that, even though he knew who both of his parents were, he was not allowed to live with them. My dad had every excuse and opportunity to sit around and feel sorry for himself but he chose not to do that. Instead, he chose to take the cards that life dealt him and fight to make the best out of them.

As a child, I was able to witness the relationship between my father and my grandfather. They were always cordial and from my perspective always glad to see each other, but it always appeared that something was missing. When I would see them greet each other it seemed as if they were distant relatives who hadn't seen each other in a long time. My grandfather would say "hello Ike," and my father would say "hey Doc." I personally believe that the ingredient that was missing was the closeness that a father and son should share due to a father's nurturing, raising, and being a part of some of his son's most important life events. Though he did not speak on it, I believe that my father longed for a close relationship with his father as he was growing up.

My older brother once told me a story that I did not remember because I was very young when this event occurred. He said that we were living in Harlem at the time and that one Sunday morning he, my dad, and I were sitting at the kitchen table. He said that my dad had just made some of his famous pancakes, which he often made when my mother had to work on Sunday mornings. There was some good ole Sunday morning gospel music playing in the background on the radio and the three of us were just sitting there laughing and talking. All of a sudden, our dad just started crying. My brother said I immediately started crying too and couldn't figure out why our dad was crying. He said after our dad had calmed down and wiped his tears away he gave us his explanation. My brother said that my dad summed it up in just three words: "I'm just happy."

I believe that my father's soul got full and heavy with happiness that Sunday morning because he sat there and fellowshipped with his sons and it felt good. He missed out on things like that with his own father as a child. I believe that is why he always made sure that he was around and that we had access to him.

From what he told me, he grew up during a time in the South when things were not really easy for African-American men. He told us that the Klu Klux Klan was prevalent and that racial tension was high in the South. He cautioned us not to fall into the trap of hatred and believe that all white people were bad, because that was not the case. He did want us to be aware of the fact that he believed that we would need to run twice as fast, as well as work twice as hard, in order to be successful in life.

My father believed that there was no substitute for hard work and always talked about how he would work around the farm. He used to tell me how he would have to go and feed the hogs on the farm and how that was a hard and messy job. He would tell us that even though it was hard work he wouldn't change anything about the experience at all. He said that having to go out and feed the hogs always kept him humble, helped to instill a strong work ethic in him, and helped to build a solid character. My father once told me that it didn't matter how big and bad he was that having to feed those hogs always brought him back down to earth. I can remember getting into a scuffle in middle school once with another kid who was picking on me just because it was Wednesday. As a result of our scuffle both of us were sent home for one day. I really dreaded the reaction that I knew I was going to get from my parents. I remember thinking on the way home "all I can do is tell them what happened." I got home and explained to my parents that this other kid started a fight with me at recess and I had to defend myself. My dad actually understood and told me that "I never want you to go looking for trouble, but if you are backed into a corner you have to defend yourself." I was happy and relieved that they understood.

The next morning my dad woke me up extra early and told me to get up and get dressed. When I was awake and had gathered my senses he said "you didn't think that you were gonna just lay around all day, did you?" Before he went to work that morning he drove me to Johns Island and dropped me off with his most trusted cousins, Ike and Bobbie Grant, who he had grown up with. He told them to put me to work. That day I realized that it wasn't cool and did not pay to get suspended from school. I cut fire wood with an axe and stacked the wood in piles the first part of the day. The second part of the day was dedicated to the same dreaded hog pen that he told me that he worked in as a child. It was horrible and I was dead tired when he came to pick me up that afternoon after he got off from work. I truly learned my lesson that day. No matter what was going on – good, bad, or ugly – he always found a way to teach a lesson.

****

When my father was about twelve years old, tragedy struck his family. His family lost everything in a house fire and no one was able to salvage any of their material belongings. What they were able to salvage was their faith in God, their family, and their determination. The family had the support of extended family members, friends, and the community but some tough decisions had to be made. The decision to stop going to school was made for him so that he could support his immediate family which consisted of his grandmother, and his younger brother, and sister. I am not really sure if he volunteered or was volun-told to take on the monumental task of supporting his family at the age of twelve, but it did not matter because my father did exactly what needed to be done. When he left school he only had a sixth-grade education, and he basically had to become a grown man overnight. There was no time for playing kick ball, baseball, going to prom, or even hanging out with kids his age, enjoying a soda pop. My father learned early on in his life how to sacrifice for others. He handled his added responsibilities with grace, dignity, and determination. I remember him telling me that "God has already written the play, and we are only following the script and acting it out." In other words everything happened for a reason, and God has everything in control. He told me that he didn't have any regrets about the life he lived and he wouldn't have changed anything about his life even if he could have. These were the amazing words of a man who only had six years of formal education and limited resources. I

HIT'EM BEFORE THEY HIT YOU

could not comprehend it as a child, but as a man I now know that was the reason that I never saw him panic, upset, or flustered. His way of thinking allowed him to calmly take on any challenges or obstacles that were placed in his path, and that set the tone for our entire family. In addition to that, I'm not sure that if he didn't think the way that he did he would have been able to keep his sanity with everything that he had to endure as a young kid.

My father came up in a different era, and in the 1930s and 1940s things were done a lot differently than they are done today. There are resources built into our society today that would provide assistance to a family in need, and make sure that a twelve-year-old would not have to shoulder the responsibilities of a grown man. By no means am I saying that my father was the only kid his age during that time who had to make sacrifices for the overall welfare of his family; what I am saying is that his amazing story of sacrifice and leadership can be used to motivate and inspire others, just like it inspired me.

As a teenager, my father worked in the fields on Johns Island, South Carolina, and did just about every odd job that he could to make an honest living and make ends meet. He picked everything from tomatoes to tobacco. Most of his friends and family called him Ike for short. He had a love for cars and had dreams of becoming a certified mechanic one day. He was very soft-spoken and did not say much. When he did speak he was very efficient, and what he said was always of importance. He was a very serious person and never wasted a breath. He had a way of unconsciously demanding the attention of everyone around him. There is no doubt in my mind that he was predestined to be a great leader, because there is no way that he could have pulled it all off without having some type of divine intervention or anointing on his life. I truly believe that people in a position of authority or leadership are called to do so, and it just doesn't happen by mistake or by chance. Besides, I do not know many twelve-year-olds who could shoulder the responsibilities that my dad had to. He was definitely forced into his leadership role, but he met and conquered the challenge head on and never complained.

My father frequently found himself in the presence of older folks, and as a result of that he gained a lot of knowledge that he would not have access to otherwise and that most other kids his age didn't get. Everyone that he came into contact with realized that there was something special about him. A lot of the older people in his community would always tell him that he had an "old soul," meaning he was wise beyond his years. He was always encouraged to do the right thing by the older folks because they felt that he was destined to do great things and didn't want him to stray off course. Being humble and listening to the advice and teachings of older folks paid major dividends for him and gave him a road map for life, which proved to be beneficial to him and everyone associated with him. There was always some type of slogan or saying that an older person in my father's life would say to him to teach him some sort of life lesson. He seemed to soak these sayings up like a sponge soaks up water. Not only did he listen to what they had to say, but if there was any way that he could apply them to his own life he did. Below is a listing of "old time" sayings that helped shape my dad into the man that he became.

He was taught early on about the **"Golden Rule"** and how he should treat people the way he wanted to be treated.

He also learned at an early age that **"manners would get you what money can't."** The older folks basically taught him that if he was always as courteous to people as he could be, then he would always be noticed by the right people and they would in turn show favor toward him. In essence, having manners is more valuable than having a pocketful of money.

My dad was told by the older people in his life that **"I would rather have friends than money."** What he took from this was that it was important to build lasting relationships with people he came in contact with in life and not take anybody for granted.

He was also taught that life was **"hard but is also fair,"** which basically means that though life may be tough nobody owes you anything. If you want something out of life you have to go out there and get it, because it is not just going to be given to you.

Ike was taught to **"be careful how you treat people on the way up, because you are going to meet the same people on the way back down."** This meant that just because you may experience a certain level of success in life, always be humble and treat those who have not been as fortunate with dignity and respect. The tide can very well turn and you could end up with the short end of the stick.

Another thing that my father was taught was that **"you never know who will have to bring you a glass**

of water." This taught him to treat everyone with respect no matter what they looked like, their social status, or where they came from, because the person you least expect may have to come to your aid.

Most importantly, my father was taught that **"Charity begins at home."** This basically meant that doing good deeds and helping people started in your own household. If you do not know how to be there to help your own family members, then how can you be ready and equipped to help a total stranger? This had a major impact on his life, and as a result he was always there for his family and friends.

He made a point to always repeat the sayings to us that he learned as he was growing up. When I was growing up I really couldn't appreciate the "old time" sayings, but as a grown man I find myself telling my kids the same things.

Due to his efforts and hard work over the years both of his younger siblings had a good shot at making it because he was able to send them to New York City to live with their mother and they both made the best out of the opportunity. He was in his early twenties when he was able to send Delores and Paul up north. My dad's younger brother, Paul, became a very successful businessman in New York City. He owned several rental properties and also owned an antique shop. His sister Delores ended up being very successful in retail business in the Boston area. They were always very grateful for his contribution to their family. He taught them the same principles that he learned as they grew older, and they never forgot where they came from.

2
The Big Apple

John 10:11 I am the good shepherd: The good shepherd giveth his life for the sheep.

My father had grown into a very responsible person and was a well-respected young man among his family members, friends, and in his community. Everyone in his community watched him grow into a young adult while feeling a sense of pride because of the sacrifices that they all knew he made as a child. On top of that, my dad had become a pretty darn good shade tree mechanic. He taught himself how to be a mechanic through trial and error, and got better at it as time went on. He started out tinkering with small engines, farm equipment, and watching the men of his community as they worked on cars. Mechanic work was really a hobby for my dad early on. He basically fixed just about everybody's car in his community under the shade tree in the front of his home. He was a very good leader among his peers and in his community but he never acknowledged it. When someone who knew his story and his background complimented him on everything that he had done he would just say, "I didn't do anything special; I just did what I had to do." That was my father's attitude regarding his role in life. He just did whatever he had to do to make things work and stayed humble during the process. He was just that guy who wanted to take care of his business, stay out of everyone's way, and work behind the scenes.

After he sent Paul and Delores up north, he missed them more and more each day. He almost always had a feeling of emptiness because he was used to having someone to take care of, and after Paul and Delores went to New York to further their education, look for work, and reunite with their mother and other siblings, he was only responsible for himself. Even though my dad and his family were separated by many miles, he still sent money up north whenever he could. As time passed he constantly got pressure from his mother and the rest of the family to pack up his belongings and move to New York. My father was very conservative, a little shy, and wanted no part of the Big Apple. He just wasn't interested in all of the bright lights, fast talking, and drama that were all part of life in the big city. Things moved too fast in the city, and he was accustomed to the slow pace of Johns Island, South Carolina.

It was 1961 when he moved to New York City to make his mother happy, because she wanted all of her children with her in the city. My dad knew that it would be a big adjustment for him but once again he thought about how much of a difference it would make for his family. They all looked up to him like some type of folk hero. He was truly a father figure to the rest of his siblings.

His transition from the quiet country life to city life went better than expected, and he quickly became the cornerstone that his family needed him to be in New York. The void that he felt was quickly filled because once again his life was dedicated to being the point man for his family. It was not always a smooth ride because his younger brothers were used to running the streets of New York and pretty much doing whatever they wanted to do. He knew that the last thing that his mother needed, to go along with her failing health, was to have to worry about her sons getting into trouble, or even worse, getting killed in the city. My dad had the difficult task of reeling his younger brothers back in to protect them from the streets as well as their own self-destruction. It took time but he was able to get through to them, mainly because he had credibility with them. The fact that they all knew that my dad was a proven leader and he would not steer them in the wrong direction helped, but it sure wasn't easy. My father's younger brothers seemed to be focused on living the fast life in the fast lane. My dad preached to them that there was no such thing as "easy money." He showed them through his own actions that they could have nice clothes, nice things, and money in their pockets if they went out made an honest living. He spent hours mentoring his brothers and staying on their cases about doing the right things. From my perspective he played more of a father figure type role instead of an older brother.

My father worked as a mechanic when he relocated to New York. The only problem was that due to his limited education he was not prepared to take the certified mechanics test. Even though he was not prepared to take the certified mechanic's test he did just as good, if not better, work than the certified mechanics he worked with. They often asked my dad for advice or input on a problem that they encountered while working on a car. In most cases he would be able to help them solve the problem, not so much because he was smarter or had more knowledge, but because he refused to let a problem beat him. He would not stop until he figured it out. Where his coworkers would get frustrated and tired of working on a problem, he would be patient, stay calm, and exhaust every effort to get the job done.

He was a good son, a good brother, and an overall good role model. He was a hard worker, a handsome man, and he was always as clean as the board of health. He had a decent job, was surrounded by family, and had everything that a young man could possibly ask for. What my father was missing was the young lady that he would spend the rest of his life with.

He soon met my mom, Frances Drye, who he instantly fell in love with. They knew some of the same people and were introduced to one another by a mutual friend. My mother was a slim but beautiful brown-skinned lady. She did not wear any makeup or have any elaborate extensions in her hair, but she was just naturally beautiful. She was working at the telephone company in New York as an operator when she and my dad met. She was not afraid of hard work at all and did not want anyone to give her any handouts. My father found the fact that she did not mind hard work very attractive, and saw her as someone he could form a life partnership with. My mom loved the fact that he was honest, he took care of his family, and he was very independent. They also had a couple of things in common that made it seem like them meeting was meant to be. My mom was also born and raised in South Carolina. She lived with her grandmother and grew up downtown Charleston. Though she loved my dad, my mom had major concerns about marrying him. My mom came from a very close-knit family, and her grandmother, who raised her, still lived in Charleston. My great-grandmother was getting older and her health was starting to decline, and my mom was afraid that if she got married she would not have the freedom to leave and go down south whenever she needed to. After Isaac consulted and had serious talks with Viola Drye, Frances's mother, and her Aunt Flourrie, he assured Frances that he would never stop her from going to her family if they needed her. Isaac received the blessing of Frances's family because they knew he was a good man and because they knew he was good for Frances.

On January 25, 1964, my parents got married and started their new lives together. My parents lived in Harlem in the projects on the fourteenth floor of their apartment building. They were not rich and they did not have everything that they wanted, but they were happy and they had each other. My older brother and I eventually were born, and my parents had the responsibility of raising two sons in the rough streets of Harlem. My brother, Isaac Bryan Waites Jr., was the oldest, and I was six years younger than my older brother. We both had a dark brown-skinned complexion like our mom. Everyone in the family called my brother by his middle name, which was Bryan. Bryan was tall and slim, and I was short and on the husky side. I was a very sickly kid. My legs were crooked so I had to wear leg braces. I was also asthmatic; the slightest amount of dust caused me to spiral into a violent asthma attack. My dad was so proud of my brother and I. He wanted to protect us, take care of us, and make sure that we did better in life then he did. He would always tell us to "reach for the sky, because the sky is the limit."

When Bryan and I were old enough we attended St. Aloysius Catholic School in Harlem. We received a quality education at St. Aloysius and had the opportunity to learn with Puerto Rican, Italian, and many other students of different nationalities and backgrounds. My parents knew that it was very important for us to get a quality education based on their own life experiences. They wanted us to do better in life, career wise, than they did. They did not mind making the sacrifice to send us to private school as opposed to public school.

Bryan and I walked about five blocks one way to get to school every morning. We were almost like Tom Sawyer and Huckleberry Finn because when the two of us traveled back and forth to and from school, there was always something going on. On our trip to school in the morning we would always walk past an alley that smelled so bad that it would make me gag as if I was about to throw up every single time. It was a foul smell that I could just never get used to. One day, while on the way home from school, we saw a man try to take a woman's grocery bag, and when she did not let the bag go the man hit her in the head with a baseball bat and busted her head wide open.

HIT'EM BEFORE THEY HIT YOU

We lived on the fourteenth floor in the projects, and some days the elevator didn't work at all. Some days it only worked a part of the way up, and then got stuck in between floors. We would then have to climb out of the top of the elevator to get out. Like I said, there was always something going on around us while we lived in Harlem.

My dad knew that the city was rough and he was extremely worried about us growing up there. He was also proud of us because we were responsible. Even though we were what some may call "latch key" kids we were accountable and stayed in our lanes. At an early age both Bryan and I knew that we had responsibilities that we had to handle for our family. We realized that both of our parents worked hard to provide for us so we had to do our part. Bryan was normally the person responsible for cleaning everything except the kitchen and bathroom. I took care of cleaning the kitchen and the bathroom. We kind of worked that arrangement out amongst ourselves without the help of our parents.

My dad was all in when it came to his family. He loved us and there was nothing that would cause us not to be together. He once told us a story about a guy he worked with at a local car garage. The man was actually his supervisor and he asked my father to do him a favor. The favor was that he wanted him to drive a package over the Brooklyn Bridge and meet someone to pick up some money. His supervisor told him that he would pay him five thousand dollars when he returned with the money he was to pick up. He knew that his family could sure use that type of money, but there was no doubt in his mind that the package that he was supposed to transport was drugs. He calmly told his supervisor that "my family is waiting for me, and I can't do that, man." He walked away from work that day, never to return to a job that he really enjoyed. There was nothing more important to him than taking care of his family. He knew that he couldn't take care of us if he was dead from a drug deal gone bad, or if he was in prison for drug smuggling. He took pride in the fact that he never handled or used any kind of drugs over the course of his entire life, and he was determined that his sons would follow that same path. He was able to find work at another garage because he was dependable and a good mechanic.

My parents were starting to feel like the city was closing in on us, and they didn't have any control over it. My dad always talked about how he grew up down south and was starting to feel that we deserved the same opportunity to breathe fresh air and go outside and play all day without having to worry about a thing. The only time that we could really go out and play in Harlem was if our dad took us out to the basketball court. This did not happen often because he worked around the clock to make extra money to support the family. He remembered when he and his family could leave home all day when he lived down south and did not even have to lock their doors.

One day Bryan and I were on our way home from school taking the same route that we always took. We were about two blocks away from our apartment building when a tall, shaggy-looking man started to follow us. He followed us all the way to our apartment building. We walked into the building only to realize that the elevator

HIT'EM BEFORE THEY HIT YOU

was not working on this particular day. We did what we normally did when the elevator was not working; we hit the stairway to start walking the dreadful fourteen floors that didn't get any easier no matter how many times we walked them. Shaggy man followed us up the stairway, but we did not realize that we were being followed until we reached about the twelfth floor. When we realized it we started walking fast, and we could then hear shaggy man start to walk fast, too. He was about one flight of stairs behind us but he was closing in on us quickly. When we reached the fourteenth floor we ran into our apartment door. We were terrified and running so fast that we never saw Shaggy man, but we could hear him. Bryan had the house key in his hand as we made our way into the apartment. As we were trying to close the door the Shaggy man stuck his left hand inside of the door, and was trying to get into the apartment. Both of us pushed and pushed, trying to keep the man out of our apartment. Somehow Bryan was able to slip away to the kitchen quickly and came back with a knife. He stabbed the Shaggy man in the hand, who automatically pulled his hand out of the doorway then we were finally able to close the door. We had seen and experienced many things while living in the Big Apple, but this incident took the cake. We didn't know if the Shaggy man wanted to rob us or kill us. We were both terrified to leave the apartment to go anywhere for a long time after that.

When my parents heard what happened they were both terrified and knew that this was the final straw. They saved every red penny that they could for the next eight months with hopes of moving down south when we got out of school for the summer. They kept this away from us not knowing how we would react to moving away from the only home we had ever known. When they saved up enough money my parents took a trip to Charleston, South Carolina, and put a substantial down payment on the house we would spend the rest of our childhood in. When the school year ended they broke the news to us and two weeks later rented a U-haul and moved our family down south to Charleston. My parents both walked away from decent-paying jobs to relocate to the south where they did not even have jobs lined up. My father was steady and knew that everything would be fine. He always had a calming presence that reassured all of us that no matter what happened everything would be okay. As a child I had no idea how big of a sacrifice that our parents made, but as I got older I realized that my parents moved so that we would have better lives. Bryan and I were not happy about moving and having to start all over again, and having to make new friends. The whole family was sad to have to leave friends and family up north, but we knew that it was time for us to start our new life.

3
Small Fry

Proverbs 22:6 Train up a child in the way he should go: and when he is old, he will not depart from it.

In Charleston, South Carolina, we moved into a modest, three-bedroom brick house in a quiet neighborhood called West Ashley. It was a stressful transition for the entire family. Both of my parents were looking for work, and things were not moving as fast as they anticipated. They had a little bit of money that they had saved for a rainy day, but since we had moved to South Carolina it seemed like it was just raining every day. Bryan really did not have any problems making new friends, because there were several kids in the neighborhood around his age range that he automatically hit it off with. I really had problems because most of the kids my age really didn't understand me. I still wore braces on my legs and suffered from severe asthma, so I could not do most of the things that the other kids did. The neighborhood kids made fun of me on a daily basis so I pretty much stayed to myself. I tried really hard to fit in, but instead of embracing me, the community kids made fun of me and shunned me away from their inner circle of friends.

On one occasion the kids in the neighborhood told me that if I wanted to be friends with them I had to complete a mission. Little did I know at the time that the mission they wanted me to complete none of them were ever able to complete themselves. The mission was to walk across a pipe that hovered over the top of a pond in the very back of our neighborhood. The pond was covered with a thick, nasty green deposit of algae and was about six feet deep. From one side of the pond to the other was about forty-five yards. I really wanted to be accepted and embraced by the neighborhood kids so I decided that I was going to do it. I was not afraid at all so I climbed up on the pipe while being watched by about eight other kids from my neighborhood. I started out walking slowly across the pipe with both of my hands spread out like I had a set of wings. I was focused, determined, and I refused to look back. Deep in my heart I knew that none of the other kids could have done this, and the thought of that made me want to complete the mission even more. I thought to myself, "If I can pull this off then they will have to let me in." I had made it three-quarters of the way across the pipe, and the onlookers actually started to get nervous because they thought that I would succeed. Up until this point they were quietly watching, but once they saw that I might make it they started making noises and shaking the pipe. This caused me to get out of rhythm and stop walking. I eventually fell into the pond, never making it to the other side, but I later discovered that I had made it farther than any of the other kids. I was able to walk and wade to the other side while the other kids just laughed. More so than anything else I was worried about how my backside would feel once my mom saw that my brand new Lee jeans and my best pair of white Pro-Keds sneakers were ruined.

There was only one kid kind enough to help me on that day and ask me if I was okay. His name was John Venable and we became great childhood friends. We did things together like catch dragonflies by the tail, shoot squirrels with BB guns, and just walk around the neighborhood. We really enjoyed each other's company. Due to John's affiliation with me he actually lost friends because everyone during this time was not warm to the idea of a black and white kid playing together. This was all new to me because I was from New York and had never really experienced any type of racism. It was fine though because it did not matter to John and me, because we decided that we were going to go against the grain and be friends anyway.

Things were looking up for the Waites family. We really had a strong support system of friends and family in Charleston. My dad was able to get a job at Sears Roebuck & Company at the local mall. Sears was about a ten-minute drive from the house for him. He was hired as a brake mechanic and worked there until his health started to fail and he had to retire. This job was important to him for several reasons. The job provided much-needed income that he needed to support our family. The job also provided health insurance and other benefits that our family needed. Most importantly, my dad was excited about the fact that this job had the potential to help him achieve one of his childhood dreams. The dream of becoming a certified mechanic was within his reach and he knew that he would at least get an opportunity to make that happen.

My mother Frances was hired to work at the Medical University of South Carolina in the Clinical Science building. She worked in the house-keeping department until she retired at the end of her career. She enjoyed her job and worked with a close-knit group of people. She had to report to work at 5:00 am so she always left home at 4:15 am. My father would get up with my mom every morning even though he did not have to get up for work that early. He would cook for her if she wanted something to eat, and rain, sleet, snow, or hail he would start her car up for her. Whenever Bryan or I left dishes in the sink from the night before, she would wake us up at 4:00 am to make sure that we took care of the dishes. She was a hard worker, a loving person, and a strict mom. Like my father she wanted us to excel and always do the right thing. She believed that we not only needed a good education, but we also needed to know about the word of God. Bryan and I were required to attend Sunday school and church on a regular basis. We were also heavily involved with the church choir, as well as the usher board.

We attended the local public schools in the area and for the most part didn't have any problems. I did get bullied at school from time to time. People tried to take advantage of me because I was soft-spoken, easy going, and tried to stay to myself. To be honest I really didn't have a high level of self-esteem or confidence in myself during that time. There was a kid named Tracy who basically bullied me at the bus stop every morning. He would just push me around for no reason. He would hit

HIT'EM BEFORE THEY HIT YOU

me, kick me, and verbally abuse me just for fun. My friend John wanted to stand up to Tracy but he was scared that he would beat him up, too. It was a well-known fact that Tracy took karate and nobody really wanted to stand up to him because everyone was afraid of him. Tracy came from a troubled home in which it was just him and his dad, and the word was that Tracy's dad was an alcoholic who verbally and physically abused his son. Obviously, Tracy took his anger and frustration out on the rest of the world. It got to the point that I would move extra slow at the house in the mornings just so that I would miss the bus on purpose, so my dad would have to take me to school.

One particular morning I went to the bus stop and Tracy was in rare form, yelling and screaming at everyone. When he saw me it seemed to have escalated his foul mood. He walked up to me and knocked my book bag out of my hand, knocking my pencils, books, and papers all over the side of the road. When I bent down to pick up my things, Tracy kicked me in my ribs like he was kicking a dog. I curled up on the ground in pain with the air knocked out of my entire body. One girl at the bus stop yelled, "Tracy, stop it!" Tracy told the girl to shut up before she got some, too. I finally managed to peel myself up off of the ground and went home. When I got home my dad was just about to leave to go to work. He could look at me and tell that I was in some type of altercation. Until then I had never told my parents about how Tracy was bullying me. I told my dad everything that was going on and I could see the pain in my father's face. Bryan was at home and overheard the conversation. He became enraged and said that he would go and take care of it. My dad stopped him and told Bryan that he was not going to do that because this was an issue that I had to deal with. My father looked at me and said "Kelvin, you are going to have to stand up to this guy." He went on to tell me that I had to stand up for myself, because until I did I would be the victim of this bully and many other bullies later in life. He reassured me that if I found myself in a situation where I had to defend myself he would support me. He took me to school that day for the last time.

The very next morning I showed up at the bus stop and Tracy started running his mouth. He never touched me but he was verbally abusive. The bus came and all of the kids got on the bus. Tracy always managed to force his way to the back seat. The only place for me to sit was two rows in front of Tracy. Tracy started by throwing paper and hitting me in the back of the head. I did a good job of ignoring it but that only made Tracy even angrier. Tracy got up and slapped me on the back of my neck. I jumped up and came around swinging in one motion and hit Tracy directly on his chin. Tracy fell back in the narrow aisle of the bus. Everybody on the bus sat there in a state of shock, including me. When I got my bearings back I leaned over Tracy and punched him one more time and told him, "I don't want to fight you, but you better leave me alone." I became cool and popular that day for not only standing up to Springfield Elementary School's worst bully, but defeating him. I was never bullied again.

As a result of my new-found fame all of the kids in the neighborhood would always stop by the house to shoot basketball or play football with me or my older

HIT'EM BEFORE THEY HIT YOU

brother. My mom constantly worried because of the braces that I used to wear on my legs, as well as the years that I suffered from asthma. Since the family moved to Charleston I got to the point where I did not have to wear the leg braces anymore, and because of the new climate my asthma seemed to fade away. A lot of my new friends played organized football at St. Andres Parks and Recreation for different teams. I was starting to figure out that I was pretty athletic, and I wanted to play organized football really bad. I asked my parents but they would not let me, because they felt that I was just too fragile. I watched my friends come and go wearing their football equipment but I knew that at least this particular year I was not going to play.

I begged my parents all summer to let me play organized football at the beginning of the next football season. My mom really did not want to let me play and had no desire to change her mind about it. My father spoke with my mother and told her that they needed to give me a chance because it sounded like something that I really wanted to do. My mom reluctantly agreed to let me play organized football at St. Andrews Parks and Recreation.

Based on the fact that I was about ten years old and had a pretty solid stature I was selected to play on a team in the Small Fry league. I was so excited about my first practice, but I was also nervous at the same time. Most of the other kids had a couple of years of experience under their belts, but this was my first ride with the rodeo. My father knew that he had to get off from work to make sure that I made it to my very first practice on time. When my father turned the corner he could see me waiting at the head of the driveway with my football uniform on and my helmet in my hand. I got in the car with my dad and off we went to the football field. When we arrived at the football field dad got out of the car but I did not. I was like a kid being dropped off at school for the first time. My father walked around to the passenger side window and said to me, "Kelvin, you can do this, just believe in yourself." I got out of the car and walked over to the football field with my father. I did not know it then but my father was just as scared, if not more, than I was. On the walk from the car to the football field I could only imagine that one thousand thoughts ran through my dad's mind. I'm sure that he thought about how I had battled crooked legs and how I had to wear the leg braces. He thought about how I suffered from asthma, and questioned rather or not I would even be able to effectively play football. He thought about how I had been bullied and my confidence level never being where it really needed to be. My father also thought about the fact that he knew absolutely nothing about the game of football. He didn't know the difference between a quarterback and a wide receiver. He was not athletic and never played any sports because his childhood was cut short. My dad felt helpless because I was about to embark on a new journey in my life and he didn't know what to tell me or how to help me.

When we made it to the football field I looked up at my dad for instructions, not realizing that he didn't know what to say. I believed in my dad and was willing to do whatever my father told me to do. What he said to me would in so many words release me from any limitations that I may have ever put on myself. It awakened and

HIT'EM BEFORE THEY HIT YOU

freed me. What my father said to me next would change my life. The only thing that he knew to tell me was to, "HIT 'EM BEFORE THEY HIT YOU." It was like what he said set me free. Nothing that happened prior to that moment mattered anymore. I started playing football on that day and did exactly what my father told me to do. During my first football season ever I played running back and linebacker and was selected as an all-star most valuable player for my football team. I was labeled as the hardest worker and hardest hitter on my team. What my father told me that day forever changed my life. It was not just about football, but it was also about life.

****

There was a new edition to our family. Terrance was my little brother and he was ten years younger than me. My parents did not plan to have any more children, but Terrance was a welcomed addition. He was the spitting image of my dad. He had his looks, complexion, and his mannerisms. I always thought that my little brother was a little spoiled. I knew that my parents were older then and didn't have the energy that they had when Bryan and I were growing up. I believed that Terrance got away with things that Bryan and I would have surely gotten a whipping for, things like talking back and rolling his eyes. Terrance was a good kid overall though; he had manners and a strong foundation to build on as he got older.

4
Razorbacks

Ephesians 6:4 And, ye fathers, provoke not your children to wrath: but bring them up in the nurture and admonition of the Lord

I continued playing football and transitioned from elementary school to middle school nicely. As I got older I began to have more confidence in myself and my level of self-esteem increased. I was very active playing football and basketball. The things that were lacking with me were good study habits and matching the intensity that I had on the football field in the classroom. I was letting my extracurricular activities and my popularity dominate my life, and was not putting in the necessary time studying that I needed to in order to be successful in the classroom. My father also noticed that I would come home and just go straight into my room, and not really spend any time around the rest of the family. This really concerned both of my parents because they had high expectations for their children. My dad was proactive and reached out to one of my teachers to find

HIT'EM BEFORE THEY HIT YOU

out what was going on in school and what my problem was. He was able to meet with my math teacher, Mrs. Polk. Mrs. Polk was a teacher from up north who had a background of dealing with at-risk youth and children from the inner city. She believed in kids working hard and fighting for their education. I knew that Mrs. Polk was passionate about education and that she genuinely cared about her students.

I remember one time that I was in Mrs. Polk's class and she was conducting a lecture. I was up late the night before talking on the phone with my girlfriend and I was feeling extremely tired. As bad as I was trying to stay awake, I kept dozing off in Mrs. Polk's class. My head was bobbing up and down like I was answering someone yes. It was a miracle that I did not break my neck. Mrs. Polk asked me to "please step outside of the classroom for a minute." When we got outside of the classroom Mrs. Polk jacked me up by the front of my shirt with both hands and pushed me up against the wall. Mrs. Polk told me, "you will pay attention in my class, and give one hundred percent, because if you don't I will call your daddy." She told me that she was willing to fight for me but she needed me to do my part. I definitely did not want her to call my father, because more than likely she would have to call him while he was at work. I knew that if my dad had to leave work to come to the school for a negative reason he would not be happy. I really respected Mrs. Polk because she had every opportunity to embarrass me in front of the entire class, but instead she pulled me out of class and treated me with respect.

Mrs. Polk did schedule a parent teacher conference

with my dad. My father took a half day off to meet with her. "Mr. Waites," she told my father, "there is no doubt in my mind that Kelvin can do a lot better than he is doing in school, but he is not giving one hundred percent." She went on to tell my father that I wanted to be ordinary in the classroom, but extraordinary on the football field. Mrs. Polk really believed that I had the talent and potential to be extraordinary in the classroom as well as the football field.

I actually sat outside of the conference room while my father met with Mrs. Polk. The meeting only lasted 20 minutes, but to me it seemed like I was sitting there waiting for two hours. I was a little scared because I knew deep down inside that I could be doing a lot better than I was doing in school. I knew that Mrs. Polk was telling my dad exactly what was going on and was not sugar-coating anything at all.

When my dad came out of the conference room with Mrs. Polk I could see the look of disappointment on my dad's face. As he walked by without making any eye contact with me he kind of mumbled to me "let's go." The ride home was very quiet, and my heart was pounding because I really thought that when I got home I was going to feel my daddy's hand on my bare backside. When we got home my dad shaved, went in and took his shower, and got himself prepared to eat dinner. While all of this was going on my mom was in the kitchen cooking dinner. After he was finished washing up everyone sat down to eat dinner, and even though my mom tried to make conversation things were a little quiet and tense. Bryan didn't even know what was going on, and he asked me if the cat had my

HIT'EM BEFORE THEY HIT YOU

tongue or something. After dinner everyone went to bed except my father and me. We sat in the den and he started the conversation by saying "Kelvin, you are better than this." He told me how both he and my mom were very disappointed with my performance in school this particular school year. My father went on to tell me that "as much as I love to see you play football, and as much as I know you love to play, you will not be playing any football this year." I looked at him in disbelief, wondering if he was bluffing to scare me or he was really being serious. During this particular time kids didn't have play stations, cell phones, or iPads. In order for my dad to really get my attention he really had to take away something that I truly loved. I thought to myself, "This cannot be happening." He explained to me that as a parent it is his job to make sure that I am focused and putting forth my best effort in school, just like it is my football coach's job is to make sure that I am ready to play on the football field. I said, "Daddy, please let me play football this year, and I promise that I will do better in school." He let me know that he and my mom had already talked about it and the decision had already been made.

I couldn't breathe and I felt like he had knocked all of the air out of my body. My dad explained to me that football was not the most important thing in life, and that my education is what I will really need in the future. He also explained to me that he believed that I was a leader and that if I was going to be a good leader I would have to do everything that I could do to take care of my business in the classroom as well as on the field. He ended the conversation by telling me that "not only are you hurting yourself, you are hurting your family, and you are hurting your team because you will not be out on the field with them the rest of the year." I was hurt and was in a state of disbelief, but I knew that I could not blame anyone but myself. I didn't play football my eighth-grade year but I was able to pull my grades up. I could not tell when I was a kid but the decision that my father made that year was exactly what the doctor ordered. The timing was perfect because I was about to go to high school, and I needed to wake up out of the daze of thinking that the entire world was centered around me. I needed to be focused on the things that were really important to my future. My father was only doing his job in getting me prepared for my very next challenge, which happened to be high school.

****

By the time I was in high school, I started to mature as a young man. I attended Middleton High School which was about five minutes away from our house. Middleton had a strong tradition of academic excellence, as well as a strong football program. Their mascot was the Razorback. Not being able to do what I loved to do the year before had given me a lot of time to reflect. I learned a valuable lesson in regards to making sure that I took care of business in the classroom, and I excelled on the junior varsity football team. That year my team went undefeated. I was still popular, people still wanted to be around me, and I still did my very best in the classroom and on the football field.

At home, things had changed for the Waites family dramatically. My older brother Bryan joined the United

HIT'EM BEFORE THEY HIT YOU

States Navy two weeks after he graduated from high school. Everybody missed Bryan when he was gone, but I believe that I missed him more than anyone else. He had been there for me my whole life. My dad was very proud of Bryan and felt a sense of accomplishment through him, because he was my dad's first son to graduate from high school and go on to serve his country. After Bryan's basic training and then his technical training, he found himself on a ship in the middle of nowhere. Bryan was now serving his country active duty in the Navy, and was now fighting in the Persian Gulf War. During this time Bryan was only able to call home about once a month. Most times it was Sunday evenings after we had made it home from church and had eaten dinner. We always looked forward to this time, and always tried to guess when Bryan would call. Then came a three-month period when we didn't hear anything from Bryan. We knew that things must have been pretty serious at the time if Bryan didn't call, because he looked forward to the calls just as much, if not more, than we did.

I remember one Sunday in particular that we were hoping that we would hear from Bryan. It was just a gloomy day all around. It was about forty-six degrees outside with a steady rain. Everyone was sitting there with our bellies stuffed, hoping that the phone would ring and we would hear Bryan's voice on the other end of the phone. Unfortunately, that call never came. All of a sudden my dad started weeping. I sat there in disbelief not knowing what to do or say. That was the only time that I can remember seeing my daddy cry. Up until that point, I truly believed that my father was some type of super hero. I believed that my father's heart had hardened over the years because of his childhood, and that he was not capable of showing emotions such as crying or laughter. On this day I realized that my father was human, and this awkward moment gave me the opportunity to do something that I had never had a chance to do. It gave me the opportunity to walk over to my dad, put my hands around his shoulders, and tell him that everything was going to be all right. My father didn't say anything but he leaned his head up against my side, and he seemed to have been comforted. I saw another side of my dad that day and he became even more of an iconic figure to me because I saw in that brief moment how much my father really cared about us. It was obvious to me at that moment that even though my dad was a strong man, he too sometimes needed encouragement.

****

I excelled in school and on the football field and I was now a senior at Middleton High School. I had plans of going to college but didn't have any idea where I would go. I knew that my parents did not make or have a lot of money, so I had hopes of getting some type of athletic scholarship to help me get into college so I could major in broadcast communications. I loved sports so much that I had dreams of becoming a sports commentator. My dad stayed on my case about doing all the right things and finishing high school strong. Football was not that important to my father, but me being a good person and a good citizen was. My mother was very concerned about me and the girls causing me not to stay focused on my school work. She would always say, "Leave them little girls alone, and keep your dang in your pants."

HIT'EM BEFORE THEY HIT YOU

I came home one day after football practice and was extremely tired. I did my homework, studied a little, and then took a shower. While I was in the shower my dad went into the dresser drawer in my room and borrowed a pair of tube socks like he often did. When he grabbed a pair of socks out of the drawer, a piece of paper fell to the floor. He picked up off of the floor what he believed to be a marijuana cigarette. The paper was rolled up tight, and was shaped like some type of cigarette. My dad instantly became enraged. He felt disappointed, angry, and did not want to believe that his son was smoking marijuana. He sat down on the side of my bed waiting for me to come out of the shower. When I came into my room I instantly knew something was wrong with my dad. He threw at me what he believed to be a marijuana cigarette. Before I could open my mouth he said "Kelvin, if I find out that you are doing drugs I will kill you." He went on to tell me that if I was strung out on drugs then I would steal and break into houses and cars to support my habit. He said, "If you are out there breaking into houses and cars then eventually somebody is going to kill you. If the homeowner doesn't kill you, the drugs will because you will probably overdose." I said, "But daddy," and as soon as I did he cut me off and said, "I don't want to hear it, Kelvin. Before I let my son die in the streets from being a druggie, I will kill him myself." Finally, I asked my dad could I please say something. My dad didn't respond, but he looked at me like, "this better be good." I said, "It's only a piece of paper with a phone number on it. I rolled it up and put it in my pocket at school. You know that mommy is always on my case about focusing on school and staying away from the girls, so I just rolled the number up to hide it from mommy." I then picked the paper up and unrolled it, and showed my dad that it was only a name and a phone number on it. My father was relieved, but all he said to me in response to the new information was, "I mean what I said about you taking drugs." I always remembered that day and how intense and passionate my father was about me staying away from drugs. As a result of that day, I never tried any type of drugs.

My dad really stayed on my case to do the right thing, especially during the summer when I had idle time. He would tell me that "Nothing good happens after dark, and I want you in the house when the street light comes on." He reminded me about how much my mother worried about me. He would say to me that "Trouble is easy to get in, but hard to get out." The only place that I would really hang out in the neighborhood was at my friend Marlin's house. Marlin lived around the corner and he was the only person in the neighborhood who had a paved basketball goal in his yard. This was a big attraction for most of the kids in the community because most of the other courts were made of grass or dirt. We would start playing around mid-day and then play until dark. I was a pretty good basketball player and would often find myself playing in the last game of the day. This game would sometimes go on 15 to 20 minutes after the street lights came on. This posed a problem for me because even though I was aware that I had a curfew, I would lose track of time, especially if I was involved in a very competitive game. I wouldn't sober up until I saw my dad turning the corner in his burgundy 225 Buick Electra. My friends would always be like, "Oh hell, here comes Mr. Waites." My father would pull up in the driveway at Marlin's house and motion with his hand for me to come over. He would never embarrass me in front of my friends, but he would always say, "Now you know your mom is worried and looking for you, Kelvin. You know that you are supposed to be home when the street light comes on." My dad would then put the car in reverse and before pulling off he would look at me and say, "You better beat me home or else we are going to have problems." I always translated that as if my dad beat me home that I was probably going to get a good whipping on my backside. If I was riding my bike, I would ride so fast that sometimes I would cause the chain to jump off. If I was on foot I would run the entire half-mile home full speed. It was not until I became a man that I realized that even though my dad was driving a car, he never beat me home. I realized as a man that my dad took no pleasure in disciplining me, but instead he just wanted me to comply and do the right thing. My father was more than happy to get his point across without having to discipline us. I realized how great of a leader my father was because of this.

Football season was over and graduation was approaching quickly for me. I really wanted things to slow down, because it just seemed as though time was slipping away so fast. I had a good football season, and was able to avoid any major injuries and stay healthy. I was offered a football scholarship to attend Newberry College in Newberry, South Carolina. My family was very proud and excited for me. My father was extremely proud due to the fact that he didn't get to finish high school, let alone have the opportunity to go to college.

As far as he was concerned Bryan and I finishing school was just like him finishing. He had pushed us to the limit and always told us to reach for the sky, because the sky is the limit. Bryan and I worked hard to be able to graduate from high school, but our dad worked even harder to provide for us and make sure that there were not any obstacles in our way that would keep us from graduating.

My original plan after high school was to join the Armed Forces and serve my country just like my older brother Bryan did. I always felt like I should have a career that focused on helping people. I often thought that when I graduated from high school I would be too young to become a police officer, so I would join the military. The only reason that I really pursued college right after high school was because I knew how bad my mom wanted me to have a college education. Being offered a football scholarship made it harder for me to tell my parents that I really didn't want to go to college at the time. I really wanted to make my family proud by being my parent's first child to go to college.

This was also an exciting time for my dad as well. He had worked very hard at Sears Auto Center for years. He was dependable, always on time, and was one of, if not the best, mechanics in the entire shop. He knew that he didn't get considered for advancement early on because he was not in the workplace clique. He would always tell us, "Just do your job, and you don't have to kiss anybody's backside. You go to work, be on time, do your best, and everything else will take care of itself." He was up for a promotion, for the first time, for a first line brake mechanic position. This promotion would

HIT'EM BEFORE THEY HIT YOU

give him more responsibility, give him a raise, and more importantly an opportunity to officially become a certified mechanic. My dad already possessed the skills to do the job, but to have that paper in his hand would be an accomplishment that he had chased his whole life. The promotion was his for the taking. All he had to do was go to a weeklong school in Decatur, Georgia, where he would be trained and his proficiency would be tested. He went to his training in Georgia and came back home to Charleston, South Carolina, as a certified mechanic. The entire family was so proud of him for his accomplishment.

****

Later that year I was preparing myself to leave home for Newberry College to start a new chapter in my life. I was prepared to leave with the foundation that my parents had given me and the determination to do anything that I wanted to do in life.

5
Newberry College

Psalm 118:6 The Lord is on my side;
I will not fear: what can man do unto me?

Football players had to report to Newberry College three weeks earlier than the other students for summer football camp. I had spent most of my summer after graduation getting myself prepared physically and mentally for the academic as well as athletic challenge that I knew that I was about to face. I had to report to the gymnasium on campus by 3 p.m. a Sunday afternoon. My parents had decided that due to convenience, the fact that I was responsible, and the fact that they trusted me they would let me drive to college my very first semester. I wouldn't have any problems finding Newberry College because I had traveled there previously for an official visit. Newberry College was actually about 2 hours and 15 minutes from Charleston.

Instead of going to church that Sunday morning my parents decided that they would take Terrance and I out to breakfast before it was time for me to get on the road and head to Newberry. My mom decided that the family would go to the local Shoney's, which was about 10 minutes away from the house. I had my 1985 Cutlass Supreme loaded down with everything that I needed to take with me to school and I planned to leave right after breakfast. I was so proud of my car and I knew that it was in tip-top shape; my dad tuned it up the week before. We all sat down to fellowship together for what we all knew would be the last time in a while. My mom blessed the food before we started to eat with a powerful prayer of protection for me. She asked that God "cover Kelvin in your blood, and put your loving arms of protection around him as he traveled the highways and bi-ways." She prayed to God that her son would stay focused, and make the best out of his opportunity. Breakfast was a little quieter than usual because everyone seemed to be suffering from some sort of pre-separation anxiety. Deep down inside my dad knew that everything would be OK with me, because I had a steadiness and calmness about me at all times. He knew for sure that I was a leader and not a follower. The highlight of breakfast that morning seemed to be Terrance playing in his food, and not really eating much of anything. I wasn't really nervous about leaving home, but I was a little sad because I had a feeling that this would probably be the last of me living with my parent's full-time. I knew that I would miss out on a lot of activities that my younger brother Terrance would be involved in as he grew older.

It was about 9:45 a.m. and I didn't want to leave any later than 10 a.m. because I wanted to drop some of my stuff off at my room before I had to report to the gym at 3 p.m. There was dead silence for about 10 minutes because it just seemed as though nobody wanted to push the goodbye button. My dad finally said, "Well, bubba, you better get going." Everyone got up from the table and they all walked outside to my dad's Buick. I hugged Terrance and said, "Be good man, and listen to mommy and daddy." I then hugged my mom, who was visibly shaken and emotional. She said, "Be careful, K, and call us when you get there." My dad and I then walked toward my charcoal gray Cutlass Supreme that was parked across the parking lot. It was weird because there was just a natural pause between us as we walked across the parking lot. It almost seemed as if that moment was parallel to the moment that my dad walked me to my first football practice. It seemed connected to the time when my father told me to "hit 'em before they hit you." I was just a little timid because I was embarking on something new, and my father was terrified because his son was once again about to do something that he had never done and he did not have any specific things to tell him about his college experience as a student athlete. Even though I knew that my father never went to college I was still looking to walk away with some wisdom from my dad just like I did years ago at the football field. I was looking for a WORD. We leaned against my car, and what was supposed to be a ten-minute conversation turned into a fifty-three-minute conversation. My mother looked across the parking lot wondering what was going on, but all she saw was my dad talking and me nodding my head. It really was a one-way conversation in which my dad broke it all down for me. The passage below is a portion of the conversation that my dad had with me before I left home for the first time to start the second chapter of my life.

HIT'EM BEFORE THEY HIT YOU

"I'm proud of you man. You have been a real good boy. You haven't given me and your momma any real trouble, and we know that we can trust you. You have overcome a lot so far in your short life, but you have not even scratched the surface of what you are destined to do. I want you to know that whatever you decide to do in life, you are good enough. Always remember to reach for the sky because the sky is the limit, and you can do anything that you set your mind to do, Kelvin. Don't ever forget where you have come from because you have a solid foundation to always fall back on as you experience life's ups and downs. I promise that you will have your share of ups and downs, but always stay calm and realize that everything happens for a reason. God has already written the play, Kelvin, and we are just following the script. Why get angry and upset about things that we have no control over? Always stay calm as you lead people or lead your family because you set the tone, and they will play off of you. Always remember to have manners because they will get you what money can't. Remember the Golden Rule and treat others like you would want to be treated.

"Kelvin, you are a leader and not a follower. Always be independent and think for yourself, and don't just follow the crowd. You may not get where you want to go in life as quickly as you want to if you stand on your own two feet, but when you finally make it you will appreciate it more, because you will know deep down inside that you didn't have to compromise yourself to get there. That's why I can look in the mirror and sleep at night.

"Be careful and take care of yourself. Don't ride

around with a bunch of guys in your car, because you can only control and know what is in your pockets and not the pockets of others. If you are out and have something to drink don't ever walk away from that drink and come back and drink it. Get a new drink! Things happen too fast and everybody you hang around with is not your friend. Believe it or not there are some people out there who don't want anything in life and are jealous about the fact that you do. They will smile in your face then try to tear you down when they think that you are not paying any attention. The sad thing is that most of the times it will be friends and family that try to hurt you. If you really think about it, Kelvin, in order to hurt someone you have to be close to them or have the opportunity to get close to them. A total stranger cannot do that. I'm not trying to scare you, but I'm just telling you things that will help you and prepare you for life away from home.

"Always stay positive, Kelvin, no matter what is going on. Always make sure that your glass is half full instead of half empty. A positive mind is a powerful thing. There is some good that can come out of every situation. Now I'm going to let you go, bubba, but I just don't feel like I would be doing my job if I didn't tell you these things. The last thing that I want to tell you is that if you want something out of life you have to go and get it. Success is not just going to knock on your door. The three things that you have to do are," he said as he counted them off on his fingers, "One: trust in God; two: work hard; and three: do something to help somebody else. I promise you, bubba, that if you do those three things you will be successful in life. I love you and God

HIT'EM BEFORE THEY HIT YOU

loves you too. I will always be with you even when you are far away. Remember to hit 'em before they hit you."

I nodded my head the entire time that my father spoke to me, but was I taking it all in. This was the longest conversation that I had ever had with my father, and it did not matter that my dad did most of the talking. I got in my car and started my journey toward Newberry College. I had plenty of time to think about all of the things that my father had told me and about my journey prior to that particular day. I thought about having to wear leg braces, having asthma, being introduced to racism, having a low self-esteem, and being bullied. I realized that I had come a long way. I was programmed by my dad to do great things. I was programmed to be confident, calm, sacrifice for others, do my personal best, and go out there and get it. So that's just what I was going to do.

****

I made it safely to Brokaw Hall at Newberry College and was directed to my dorm room, which was located on the second floor. I met my roommate, Terrell, who was from Greenwood, South Carolina. We briefly spoke about the respective positions that we both play. I raved about playing strong safety and how much I loved the game of football. Terrell talked about playing the wide receiver position. Terrell was about six feet two inches tall and it appeared that he didn't have any more than two percent body fat in his whole body. He reminded me of a greyhound. We were both freshmen and hit it off from day one. We both unpacked a little and then walked over to the gym together. When we reached the gym we were both in awe of how everyone seemed to be well put-together athletes. It was intimidating to me because everyone inside of the gymnasium appeared to be an elite athlete. I knew that I would have to work twice as hard as everyone else to even be able to set foot on the field. Summer conditioning started right away and continued for two weeks. I honestly believed that Newberry was the hottest place on the planet. Training camp was tough and I had never trained so hard in my life before because I had always gotten by with pure determination and natural athleticism. I was really not into weight lifting much when I was in high school so it was an adjustment I had to make quickly at Newberry. I was so dehydrated one night in my dorm room that I cramped up from my neck all the way down to my hamstrings. Terrell called the athletic trainer who realized that I had not been taking in enough fluids during the two-a-day workouts, and decided that I needed to have an IV. Even after that, it didn't matter how tough things got, I told myself that I was not going to quit. I wanted to prove to myself that I belonged there and that I could compete on a collegiate level.

I made it through the conditioning part of summer camp and then Newberry was preparing for its very first game of the season. We were going to travel down to the South Carolina State Bulldogs in Orangeburg for our first game of the season. Classes had started by this point and I was getting a big dose of what it meant to be a student athlete. The team was practicing two times a day, having team meetings, and requiring us to attend study hall at the end of each day. Most evenings when I finally made it back to my dorm room I was dead tired. I

HIT'EM BEFORE THEY HIT YOU

was doing my best to adjust to the commitment of being a collegiate student-athlete and on the football field I was starting to separate myself from my freshman class, and actually had a chance of getting some playing time once the season started. At most practices I literally had to fight because the upperclassmen were not overly excited about a freshman coming in and earning playing time. There was also controversy brewing among the coaching staff concerning me and my playing time. The head coach, who actually recruited me out of high school, was impressed with the way I played the safety position. He often told the other coaches that "this kid plays with passion and a sense of urgency." The defensive coordinator felt the same way but he was not keen on the idea of a freshman starting or even getting moderate playing time. He didn't believe that I was ready to start and was partial to the senior safety who had started the two previous seasons.

The drama started when the head coach told the defensive coordinator that he would like to see me start, but it didn't happen. When our defense took the field against South Carolina State University in our first game of the season I was not on the field. After my head coach realized that his orders had not been followed I could feel the stress and tension among the coaching staff. The only reason that I knew what was going on was because my head coach came to me personally during the game. "I hope that you are ready to play, Kelvin, because I have confidence in you," he said. "You are good enough, now don't let me down." I was put into the game during our third defensive sequence, and played the rest of that game.

I took my coach's words to heart and played my heart out. I finished my first college game with four tackles and one pass deflection. The fact that my coach not only believed in me, but stuck his neck out for me, meant a lot to me. I started every other game the rest of the season at safety for the Newberry Indians. Unfortunately, the defensive coordinator was fired around mid-season. Newberry did not have a winning season this particular year, but I was awarded with the Defensive New Comer of the Year Award.

My sophomore year was a lot different. The president of the college decided to go in a different direction with the football program. The word on the street was that the team lacked discipline and the president of the college didn't have confidence in the former coach to get the team where it needed to be in that area. An almost entirely new coaching staff was brought in a couple of weeks before summer camp, which was a complete surprise to the entire football team. This move caused a high level of anxiety and frustration among all of the football players. The only coach left from the previous coaching staff was the defensive backs coach. All the defensive backs on the team, including myself, were happy with this decision, because at least there was someone left behind on the coaching staff who knew what we all could do. There were still no guarantees because the new coaching staff had the responsibility of evaluating every player and their positions and did not have much time to do it. On top of that, the players had to learn totally different offensive and defensive schemes, rendering the playbooks that we had taken home over the summer obsolete. The new coaching staff

HIT'EM BEFORE THEY HIT YOU

put a lot of emphasis on the basics. They focused on fundamentals and conditioning. It was almost as if they were tearing down the frame of an old house or some sort of structure with hopes of rebuilding it. The only thing that they left in place was the foundation.

Summer camp went fine for the team as the coaching staff and players were both becoming familiar with each other's expectations. It was a totally different philosophy than what the former coaching staff preached. The former coaching staff felt that it was important to know the backgrounds and family life of all their players. They thought that before they ask a student-athlete to buy into what they were doing and go to war with them, then they needed to know the actual person. This went a long way with the players the former year, because it actually made them feel like they were a part of a team as well as a family. The new coaching staff's main focus was X's and O's. They were not really concerned with the background of the players. According to them, you did what you were supposed to do or you did not step on the field. The players took a while to get used to this concept. There definitely was not a lot of nurturing going on, and it didn't feel like a family atmosphere to me. The Newberry Indians won five games that year and lost six.

I felt totally different after football season during my sophomore year. I just didn't have the fire and desire to be there anymore. I had started to feel restless and out of place in Newberry and the stress of being a student-athlete was really wearing me down.

During the spring of my sophomore year, I was talking with an Army recruiter on a regular basis, and had yet to discuss what I was thinking with my parents. I finally made up my mind that the upcoming summer I would enlist and go to basic training at Fort Jackson in Columbia, South Carolina. Prior to telling my parents what my plans were, I decided that I wanted everything in place and etched in stone so that it would be harder for anyone to talk me out of it. I took the Armed Services Vocational Aptitude Battery Test (commonly known as ASVAB) at the Military Entrance Processing Station (MEPS) at Fort Jackson. Based on my test scores I was able to choose the job that I preferred to do in the Army. I decided that I would be a Morse interceptor in the military intelligence field. The job description excited me and the fact that I would need to obtain a top-secret security clearance excited me even more.

Before I went home for the summer I advised my position coach as well as the head coach that I would not be returning to Newberry College the following year. I advised them that I had plans of going a different direction with my life and I would be enlisting in the U.S. Army. This was a total shock for the coaching staff because I had started for the past two seasons and was a decent student. The way that my head coach responded to the news only confirmed to me that I was doing the right thing. The first thing out of the head coach's mouth was, "Son, you are going to set me back in recruiting." I thought to myself, "Wow, all he has to say is I'm setting him back in recruiting." The coach did not ask if I was okay or if my family was okay back home in Charleston. All he cared about were X's and O's. It was all a numbers game. I had a desire to be a part of something special and that something special I decided was the U.S. Army.

HIT'EM BEFORE THEY HIT YOU

When I went home that summer I immediately asked my parents to sit down so that I could talk to them about my plans. When I broke the news my mom became very upset. All she could think about was me going to war. She couldn't wrap her head around why I would want to walk away from a football scholarship at a good college. My mom totally shut down and did not hear anything that I had to say after I told them that I was enlisting. She was so upset that she left the room saying, "Isaac, you better talk to him." My dad was slow to speak as always and he let me tell him exactly how I felt. I told my father that I really wanted to go into the Air Force before I decided to go to Newberry, but I didn't want to let everyone down. I also told him that I truly believed that I was supposed to follow a career path of service, and choosing to join the United States Army would be the beginning. He responded by telling me, "Bubba, I have always told you to think for yourself. You have to live your own life, and your mom or I can't do it for you. I support you in whatever you want to do, and don't worry about your mom because she is just afraid of the possibly of you having to go to war."

I felt better after that and as the time passed my mom calmed down a little. I had two weeks to get myself mentally prepared for the newest challenge of my life.

6
Basic Training

Isaiah 41:10 Fear thou not; for I am with thee: be not dismayed; for I am thy God: I will strengthen thee; yea, I will help thee; yea, I will uphold thee with the right hand of righteousness.

Before I knew it, it was mid-August and time for me to report to Fort Jackson for basic training. My family drove me to Columbia, South Carolina, to drop me off. It was a very quiet ride; my mom still wasn't too happy about my decision, but she knew deep down inside that she had to accept it. She prayed that everything would work out for me and that God would protect me during my basic training. I was a little nervous only because I really didn't know what to expect. In terms of the physical challenge I was certain that I wouldn't have any problems meeting the challenge, even though I hated long-distance running. I planned to motivate myself by telling myself, "If I can play football in college at a high level for two years then I should be able to make it through basic training." I did not take the challenge lightly at all, but I did have the calm voice of Isaac Waites in my head telling me that everything would be okay. I acknowledged that I would be challenged mentally, and that I would have to learn how to work with and depend on those I would be training with from around the country. I knew that the drill sergeants would be on us day and night, pushing us to the limit physically and mentally. I had a plan to say to myself: "They can make me do push-ups and run all day, but they cannot eat me." I was excited about the opportunity to serve my country, and felt like my life was really starting to have a purpose.

Once we arrived at Fort Jackson, my family and I were directed to an area set aside for family and friends to visit with the soldiers before it was time to say final goodbyes. It was a nice atmosphere, and the active duty military personnel present were caring and supportive. Before everyone realized it, it was time to say goodbye. My mom hugged me and said, "Remember what your Aunt Ada told you when you were younger," and I hugged my mom in agreement. When I was younger, my Aunt Ada told me that I was going to be somebody one day, even though the devil would try me. Aunt Ada was my grandmother's sister and I spent a lot of time around her when I was younger. She was very wise and well respected by her family, friends, and the community. I learned a lot from her, and she always believed that I would make a difference in many lives one day. While my mom was still hugging me, she whispered in my ear. "Never forget the 23rd Psalm. I don't care where you are or what you are doing, you can always say 'the Lord is my Shepherd I shall not want.'" I nodded my head and then faced my father.

"Bubba, you have to live your life," he said. "Go out there and get it, and watch your back. Continue to reach for the sky and know that you can do anything that you want." He reminded me of the three things in life that I needed to do to be successful. "Always trust in God, work hard, and do something to help somebody else." The last thing he told me was that "I'm proud of you and you have my blessing." My fiancé Chelice hugged me like she was never going to see me again. We had plans of getting married after I completed basic training and my advanced training at Fort Devens. We met my freshman year at Newberry College at a fraternity party, and I told her when we met that we would be getting married one day. She blew me off then by saying "I don't think so" but we eventually started dating. The Army personnel then started to guide us to the buses so that we could be bused to our respective companies.

As I sat on the bus I looked toward the front of the bus and saw the drill sergeant step on. He smiled at all of the soldiers and told us to wave at our families and tell them goodbye, and just about all of us were hanging out of the windows doing just that. As the bus turned the corner and was out of the sight of the soldiers' families and friends, the drill sergeant's demeanor changed. "Good morning, my name is Drill Sgt. Davis and I am in charge of B Platoon. Forget about your moms, your pops, and your girlfriends because Jody has your girlfriends now. Put your damn heads between your legs and I don't want to see any of your eyes until I tell you to look up. Play time is over and all of your asses belong to me."

HIT'EM BEFORE THEY HIT YOU

Drill Sgt. Davis was an intimidating specimen of a man. He wore his campaign hat so that you could barely see his eyes. He had dark smooth skin and a very deep voice. He was about six feet, three inches tall, and appeared to weigh about two hundred and forty pounds. He was shaped like a professional football player. You could have heard a pin drop on the bus, and most of us were in a state of shock. I stayed calm, as usual, but was wondering what would happen next and what in the hell I had gotten myself into.

As the buses arrived at their respectable company areas there was a manufactured atmosphere of confusion and panic. The drill sergeants were yelling and screaming at us to quickly get our gear and line up in formation. If they said it once they said it a thousand times: "I got all day to wait on you, private!" It was obvious to me that everyone was moving as fast as they possibly could, but it didn't matter because we would get yelled at either way. I kept saying to myself, "They can't eat me. They can't eat me." After we all lined up in formation we were given instructions on what squads we would be in and what would happen next. We were taken to get haircuts and were issued everything that we would need: hats, gloves, socks, camouflage uniforms, and boots. All of us were then escorted to the Post Exchange to get any toiletries we may need. The drill sergeants were stalking us to make sure that we didn't put any snacks in our bags. Drill Sgt. Davis said, "Please be the one to let me catch you with chips, cookies, or candy or any other crap in your bag. If I catch any of you scally waggs with that junk I will smoke you until you can't move." Smoking meant that the drill sergeant would have us do push-ups, sit ups, legs raises, or any other exercise that he could think of until our body physically couldn't take it anymore and went into muscle failure.

For the first three to four weeks of basic training nobody in my company could do anything right. It was by design and the drill sergeants were purposely making our lives a living hell. They would smoke us until we couldn't walk and then only allow us to sleep for a few hours at a time. They wanted to push us to our physical and mental limits. They wanted us to get rid of the idea that we were a group of individuals and wanted us to learn the true importance of being a part of a team. They were on our cases constantly, to the point that the drill sergeants didn't give us any time to even breathe.

For a brief moment while sitting in the chow hall one day I wondered "What in the hell am I doing here? Last year this time I was at Newberry College on a football scholarship." I questioned whether or not I had done the right thing by leaving school and enlisting in the Army. I questioned whether or not I had taken full advantage of the opportunity that I was given. Even though I remembered my father's teachings and knew that everything happened for a reason, I couldn't help but think that I had made a major mistake by leaving school and joining the Army. I had been day dreaming for about ten minutes, and when I came back to my senses Drill Sgt. Davis was standing right in front of me. "Private Waites, since you have so much time to day dream you are finished eating." He didn't even give me a chance to eat or drink anything on my tray that morning and that really got to me. I told myself that it was only a test and things would get better soon.

HIT'EM BEFORE THEY HIT YOU

The second part of my basic training experience got a lot better. This phase focused on marksmanship, field exercises, long road marches, and drilling. Before I knew it graduation from basic training was a couple of days away. We had all made it. Even though we all had different orders to attend follow-up training at different training bases all over the country, we realized that we would be connected somehow for the rest of our lives. We all shared blood, sweat, tears, pain, and plenty of laughs together.

****

Graduation had come and gone and I had a two-day break before I was scheduled to report to Fort Devens in Massachusetts. I didn't know much about Fort Devens other than it was the Military Intelligence Headquarters and that it got extremely cold there during fall and winter months. I spent time with my family, catching up, and eating good food for about twenty-four hours before I had to fly to Logan Airport in Boston.

I arrived at Logan Airport in Boston at about 3:30 p.m. on a Saturday afternoon. I was surprised to see the size and condition of the airport. I had never been to Boston before and was really expecting Logan Airport to be something like Atlanta's airport. I was expecting something a lot larger and more modern. I collected my luggage and walked down the steps and as soon as I got to the bottom of the steps I found myself outside in the snow. I immediately flagged down a taxi cab that would transport me to Fort Devens, which would be my new home for the next six to twelve months. It was the beginning of November and I was being introduced to the harsh, cold weather of New Hampshire. It was snowing and the roads were very icy. The weather reminded me of growing up in Harlem, but it was worse. As I was riding down the interstate in the cab I saw a sign that said WORCHESTER EXIT. I read it out loud and the cab driver heard me say "WOR-CHEST-ER." The cab driver immediately corrected me and told me that the way that I pronounced the word was not the correct pronunciation. If I was going to fit in and be welcomed with open arms to Massachusetts then I would have to learn how to talk. He told me that even though Worchester was spelled the way it was, the correct pronunciation is "WIS-STER." I was thankful that the cab driver got me straight on that before I repeated it to anyone else and made a fool out of myself.

I finally arrived at Fort Devens and was directed to my barracks room where I was able to get settled in.

I was happy to begin my training. I was ready to learn the job that I would do for the duration of my military career. I was proud to be training at the Military Intelligence Headquarters for the U.S. Army. The atmosphere at Fort Devens was totally different from the atmosphere at Fort Jackson. It was more relaxed. We still did physical training three times a week, but we were off on the weekends to come and go as we pleased. By the time the weekend rolled around all of us trainees were ready to let our hair down, take a break, and have some fun. The first part of the training consisted of the trainees learning Morse Code, which was not an easy thing to do. It was like learning a whole new language all over again. Training during the week was pretty serious and intense. The instructors told the trainees early in the course that this particular job had the highest suicide rate in the U.S. Army at that time. When I heard that I couldn't help but think to myself, "What a vote of confidence." All of us in the Morse Interceptor course were all required to have a top-secret security clearance and were not allowed to openly talk about their specific jobs and the different technologies that we used to do our jobs. Getting a top-secret security clearance was a very tedious process. The government actually went back to my community and interviewed some of my neighbors, as well as my elementary school teachers. I was really challenged by the program and was successfully approaching completion. I knew that I was close to finishing up my training because I received orders for my first duty station. I received orders to go to Korea for one year after my training at Fort Devens. I was not really happy to get orders for Korea because I had hopes of getting married after I finished my training at Fort Devens. The duty station in Korea does not allow for family members to accompany soldiers, which would mean that I would be away from my wife for about one year. This troubled me so I called my father just to vent about it a little bit. There was no hesitation or any doubt in my mind that orders were orders and that I would do what I was ordered to do. When I told my father my dilemma he assured me that everything would be okay, because everything happens for a reason. "The Lord works in mysterious ways, bubba." He assured me that if I had to go to Korea for a year he would make sure that my wife was taken care of.

Two weeks before I finished my training I was called to the First Sergeant's office. When I got the message I was trying to figure out what did I do to get in trouble, because nobody ever got called to the First Sergeant's office for anything good. I wondered if I had talked trash to an officer or something while playing basketball in the gym. I was so competitive and I was always running my mouth on the basketball court or in the gym. I just figured that I may have rubbed somebody the wrong way and it was catching up with me. The First Sergeant seemed to be in a good mood when I arrived. As soon as I walked in he handed me an envelope and told me to open it and read it. I opened the envelope and to my surprise it contained updated orders for my duty station after my advanced training. The orders basically told me that instead of being stationed in Korea for one year I would be spending the next three years in Augsburg, Germany. I jumped in the air and shouted "Yes, thank you so much First Sergeant!" My First Sergeant replied by saying, "Don't thank me PFC Waites, I didn't have anything to do with this. Either you have a rabbit's tail in your pocket, or you are the luckiest man that I have ever met." I didn't respond but deep down inside I knew that it wasn't by chance that my orders had changed, but it was the work of the Lord. I finished my training at Fort Devens and flew home to Charleston for ten days of leave before I had to fly to my next duty station.

7
Augsburg

*Hebrews 13:8 Jesus Christ the same
yesterday, and to day, and for ever.*

I arrived at the Charleston International Airport and felt like Dorothy from the Wizard of Oz. I thought to myself, "There is truly no other place in the world like Charleston, South Carolina." I was so glad to be back home, even if it was just for a few days, that I could have kissed the ground. I really enjoyed the training that I had just gone through at Fort Devens, but I was not going to miss the weather. All of my family was waiting for me at the airport and were so happy to see me. They drove me to my parents' home where more family awaited so that they could celebrate my return. The family decided that since we did not have much time to celebrate after my basic training then they would celebrate before I went to my next duty station. I was greeted at my parent's home by friends and family. There were plenty of hugs, laughter, and good food. There was fried chicken, fried fish, barbecued ribs, macaroni and cheese, collard greens, candy yams, and many more goodies. This was the best celebration that I ever had. I took this time to let my family know that I would not be going to Korea again, but instead I would be going to Augsburg, Germany. Everyone was happy, but the news really didn't affect anyone more than my fiancé. She was so excited at the fact that we would be getting married in a few days and at some point she would be able to join me and start our new life and family together in Europe. Time moved extremely fast over the course of my ten days at home. I had a lot of personal business to take care of and I also got married during this time. Chelice and I had a small wedding with only our closest family and friends attending.

Ten days at home seemed like two days at home and I found myself at the airport once again saying goodbye. I was starting to become pretty good at saying goodbye. I decided from that point on that I was not going to say goodbye, but instead I would say "See you all later." My wife, mom, dad, and little brother all accompanied me to the Charleston International Airport one more time to see me off. Chelice would travel to Germany two months after I did. I hugged and kissed my wife and hugged everyone else. My mom and Chelice were too emotional to say anything. My dad shook my hand and pulled me close and hugged me. "Well bubba, no long speeches because you know what to do. Work hard and always take care of your family." As I turned to walk away my dad said, "Hit 'em before they hit you, bubba." I boarded the plane and was off to Fort Worth, Texas, where I would change flights and then fly into the Munich Airport in Germany.

My flight made it to the Fort Worth Airport safely,

and I had a two-and-a-half-hour layover before my next flight. While I sat in the airport awaiting my flight there was a couple sitting directly in front of me. They were wearing their U.S. Army uniforms just like I was. They both had the name Davis on the name tags on their uniforms, and it was obvious that they were married. The gentleman was a clean-cut, dark-skinned African-American male, and his wife appeared to be of Latin descent. I was in my early twenties at the time, and the couple appeared to be in their early forties. The gentleman spoke to me saying, "Hey man, you headed to Augsburg too, huh?" I nodded. Staff Sergeant Davis said, "Yeah this will be me and my wife's second tour there." He could see by the rank on my uniform that more than likely this was my first duty station. We chatted back and forth for a couple of hours before we boarded the plan. Once we boarded the plane we sat directly across from each other and continued our conversation. We talked about everything from family to each of our favorite football teams. Both Marvin and I were Dallas Cowboys football fans, which caused us to hit it off like we had known each other for years. Our families would become great friends and would spend the next three years together in Germany.

When I arrived at the Munich Airport and maneuvered my way through customs and then baggage claim, I lost track of Marvin and Nena. While I was walking through the airport I thought to myself, "These German police officers look pretty serious about what they are doing." I noticed that none of them smiled, made eye contact, or greeted me as I walked through the airport. I waited around, hoping to bump into any Army personnel,

KELVIN WAITES

because I was told that someone would be there to pick me up. About three hours went by and nobody ever showed up to pick me up, and I had no idea who to call. "This is a hell of a way to start my tour of duty in Germany," I thought. Then I noticed a guy walking toward me, looking at me strangely. The gentleman had long brown matted hair and an equally long matted beard. His eyes were bloodshot red and he was dirty. He appeared to weigh at least three hundred and fifty pounds. When he got right up on me he said, "Hey, bo you going to Augsburg? 'Cause I can give you a ride if you need one." I remember thinking to myself, "There is no way in hell that I'm about to ride anywhere with this guy." The man told me that his name was Ronnie and that his wife was in the Army stationed in Augsburg, and he just put her on a flight to go San Diego. He asked me to excuse his appearance because he is a mechanic and he had been working on cars all morning prior to bringing his wife to the airport. He told me that he was going to Augsburg and he didn't mind giving me a ride. Augsburg was about fifty minutes away from the Munich Airport. Ronnie said, "Dude I know that I look like the one man gang, but you can trust me to give you a ride to Augsburg." I thought that I might as well take a chance and get the ride because I had run out of options. Ronnie walked me to his metallic blue mid-eighties Dotson hatchback. He was almost just as big as the car. We jumped on the Autobahn and headed toward Augsburg. Ronnie talked all forty-five minutes of our short trip. It was okay though because I was so amazed by the country side and its beauty that I didn't pay Ronnie much, if any, attention. I had never seen fields so green in my life and I thought to myself that the landscape had to be sculpted by God himself. Once we arrived on post Ronnie dropped me off at headquarters and went on his way. I was very appreciative of the ride and tried to give Ronnie some gas money. He wouldn't take the money. "Bo, we was going in the same direction and it was not a problem at all."

I checked in at headquarters and found out that they were not expecting me for another month, which is why nobody was at the airport to pick me up. The headquarters personnel could not stop apologizing to me for the confusion and inconvenience. I was issued my room in the barracks and given some time to get settled in. After a while I heard a knock at my barracks door and it was a soldier at the door named Specialist Kelvin Gilliam. He was about five feet, six inches tall and weighed about one hundred and forty-five pounds. He said, "Hey man, that was my bad, because I was the one who was supposed to pick you up." He told me that everyone called him Gill and he was from North Carolina. Gill showed me around post and showed me where I would be working for the next three years. Everyone appeared to be so nice on the military post in Augsburg. It was a very close-knit military community where everybody knew everybody. I was introduced to the members of my company and command staff by Gill and was given a tour of the top-secret facility where I would work every day. I would be working at a facility called Gablingen Kaserne. It was a secure location where the military intelligence personnel worked out of in Augsburg. It was a high-tech facility and I could not wait to get to work. I was astonished by how friendly the local Germans were and it seemed to me that the Germans were really in support of the soldiers being there. I was also impressed with the relaxed atmosphere of being at my regular duty station. Unlike basic training at Fort Jackson and advanced training at Fort Devens, it really seemed like you just went to work, did your job, and went home to your family.

****

Two months had passed and I was getting into the swing of things. I was well known among my peers and spent a lot of my free time hanging out and shooting basketball or playing racquet ball at the gym. I moved into my off-post housing in anticipation of my wife Chelice arriving. I had everything set up for her and was ready to start our life together in Europe. Chelice made it to Germany wondering what her life with her new husband would be like in Europe away from family and friends. We had so much fun together getting to know one another and soon our first born, Jasmin, popped up on the scene. Chelice, Jasmin, and I really grew as a family. We were thousands of miles away from our loved ones, but we had each other to lean on.

Chelice decided that she was going to go back to college to finish up her college education at the University of Maryland's European Division. This was a trying time for our young family because I was on permanent graveyard shift. As I would come dragging in the door after a night of work and physical training the following morning, Chelice would hand Jasmin off to me. I could only pray that Jasmin, who wasn't even a year old, would cooperate and let me sleep a little while.

HIT'EM BEFORE THEY HIT YOU

I would normally arrive at our apartment eight minutes after eight, and Chelice would have to be in class by eight thirty. I knew that it was a family sacrifice, but in the end it would all pay off.

We had been in Germany for a couple of years and had an extended family of close friends that we enjoyed fellowshipping with on a regular basis. I spent a lot of time hanging around with Marvin Davis, as well as Gill. I really enjoyed my job and all of the soldiers I worked with. I had become one of the best Morse Code Interceptors in my company at developing new targets. My job as a Morse Interceptor was to copy the Morse Code that countries unfriendly to the United States transmitted. We monitored these countries every day, twenty-four hours a day, and copy their coded and un-coded messages. Chelice enjoyed talking with and taking trips with the other Army wives to different tourist attractions around Europe.

During this time there was also a new addition to our family. My son, Kelvin Anthony Waites, Jr. was born. We decided that we would call him K.J. Chelice and I were extremely happy that God had blessed us with two beautiful, healthy children. We had grown as a family and had learned how to depend and count on one another. I had always told myself that if I ever had kids that they would know that I was dad, but I would also be their friend. I was so appreciative of everything that my parents had done for me, but when I was younger there was really no time for my parents and I to really become friends. It may sound weird but my parents stayed busy working and providing for our family and there wasn't time to go bowling, to the movies, or do a lot of fun stuff. It was all about getting your school work done, keeping the house clean, and going to church. My parents just didn't have time for a lot of extracurricular activities, but they found a way to take care of us and keep us on track. My goal was to raise my children on the same principles that I was raised on, but to also be able to get on their level to understand the things that they would face in their everyday lives.

About a month after K.J. was born I received a disturbing message from the Red Cross concerning my father. The message was that my dad had suffered a heart attack and was being treated at the Medical University of South Carolina in Charleston. I was surprised, very concerned, and all I could do was figure out how I was going to get to my dad. Chelice, the kids, and I took a flight on an Air Force cargo plane out of Ramstein Airbase in Germany about twenty-four hours after getting the news. The plane was scheduled to stop at a military air base in Delaware, and then we would pick up another flight that would fly into the North Charleston Air Base in South Carolina. We arrived in Delaware only to be held over for twenty-four hours because the flight that was going to North Charleston had been cancelled. We arrived at the Charleston Air Force Base the following day and went straight to the hospital. I walked into my father's room to find him lying in his hospital bed with tubes and wires spread all over his body. He didn't even realize that I was there. Prior to my arrival the doctors had given him medication to make sure that he rested and was comfortable. My mom was actually praying when I walked in the room and she didn't even notice that I was there. When my mother

HIT'EM BEFORE THEY HIT YOU

opened her eyes she saw me standing there and all she could do was shout "Halleluiah!" She was happy I had come all the way from Germany to see about my father. My mom embraced me and couldn't help but just hug me and cry. She kept saying, "Kelvin, your daddy is a strong man, but he is having a hard time." She told me that his symptoms indicated that he had a heart attack but they can't get any good readings on his vitals. She went on to tell me that because of this the doctors were skeptical about any types of surgery but they had him prepared to have an MRI done to get an indication as to what was really going on. While I stood at the foot of my father's bed holding my mom the technician came in to get my dad ready to go take him for his MRI. Before we knew it they had quickly taken him out of the room. While we waited for him to return my mother was telling me how my father was calling for me, and she was just afraid that I would not make it there in time. Even though she was very strong in her faith she was visibly shook and needed me there for support. I told my mom that "God has everything under control, and daddy will be okay because he is a fighter."

About an hour later the technicians brought my dad back to the room. He was still heavily sedated. The two technicians diligently got him settled back into his room and they told us that the doctor would be in to speak with us about the results of the MRI shortly as they left the room. Fifteen minutes after the technicians left a team of three doctors entered the room to discuss the results of my father's MRI and update us on the game plan that they would be taking to get him better. All three of the doctors appeared to be of Indian origin, and

71

their body language indicated to me that they may have good news. The lead doctor said, "Mrs. Waites, I wanted to give you some information regarding your husband's ailments." We both listened to the doctor attentively as he explained that my dad had three blockages but he assured us that they had them under control. The doctor went on to explain that the reason it took them so long to diagnose his condition was because he is a very special and unique man. "Your husband has a condition called Situs Inversus," the doctor said to my mother. "The condition consists of someone's organs being on the opposite side of their body. For example, someone who has the condition of Situs Inversus would have their heart on the right side instead of the left, with all of their other organs switched as well. Your husband is a very unique person because only 0.01 percent of the population have this condition. This condition is what threw off all of the readings on the instruments, because the instruments were made to gauge and read the vitals of a person with a normal body. It was only by the grace of God that he did not die before we found out that his organs were on the wrong side of his body."

The doctor assured my mom that they would do a procedure to place a stint in his heart and he would be okay. The hospital staff did not waste any time in performing the surgery so my dad could start his recovery process.

8
Decisions

Proverbs 3:5-6 Trust in the Lord with all thine heart; and lean not unto thine own understanding. In all thy ways acknowledge him, and he shall direct thy paths.

Chelice, the kids, and I spent the next thirty days in South Carolina visiting with family and friends. My dad was recovering slowly and had already started physical therapy. We tried to spend equal time with my family in Charleston as well as Chelice's family in Georgetown. During my time home I did a lot of thinking about how my parents were getting older and I was so far away. I really didn't like the helpless feeling that I had when I was trying to make it to South Carolina to get to my father. I had one year left in the military to fulfill my four-year obligation and I was seriously thinking about not re-enlisting and moving a little closer to home. I was in Georgetown one day and bumped into Chelice's brother-in-law. His name was Isaac Pyatt and he was a lieutenant at the local sheriff's office. Isaac was working on this particular day and asked me to come and ride with him for a little while. Isaac took me on a tour of Georgetown County. I was amazed by the size of the county, and was impressed with Isaac's knowledge and professionalism regarding his job. After my tour of the county was over Isaac took me back to the actual sheriff's office to show me around the building and introduce me to some of the men and women he worked with. It became very clear that Isaac was recruiting me to come back to Georgetown when I got out of the military to become a deputy sheriff. Isaac introduced me to a few people who were hanging around the patrol room. When we were about to leave a man walked in the room and Isaac said, "Hey, Sheriff." He introduced me to Sheriff A. Lane Cribb. After greeting Isaac and I, Sheriff Cribb said, "Isaac, ya'll come on back." As we were walking back to the sheriff's office I thought to myself, "The sheriff looks like somebody's uncle." He was about five feet, seven inches tall, a little on the husky side, brown hair, and he appeared to be in his mid-fifties. The three of us walked back to Sheriff Cribb's office and Isaac went to take care of some paperwork and left Sheriff Cribb and I alone to talk. Sheriff Cribb asked me "What exactly do you do in the Army and where are you stationed?" I told the sheriff that my job was to copy Morse Code that countries who were not friendly to the United States transmitted. Sheriff Cribb said, "Hmm, that sounds pretty high tech." I even told him about how I had to have a top-secret security clearance in order to do my job. He seemed to be fascinated about my clearance, and told me "Well if I decide to hire you one day, I won't have to do so much of a background check because Uncle Sam has already done most of it for me."

HIT'EM BEFORE THEY HIT YOU

He then winked at me. He really seemed to be interested in what I had to say. I soon turned the conversation around and was picking the sheriff's brain about his job. "Sheriff, what do you like the most and the least about your job"?

"The thing that I don't like about my job is when I have to tell a parent or loved one that their child or loved one has died, but what I love most about my job is that I get to help people," he responded. I was intrigued by what the sheriff was saying and valued every word that came out of his mouth. Sheriff Cribb seemed to be a very intelligent man and I was impressed. He asked me what my plans were regarding the military and if I planned on staying in for twenty years. I told the sheriff that "My father is sick, and I am truly debating on whether or not I am going to get out of the Army or re-enlist." What he told me next would be something that I would remember for the rest of my life. The sheriff looked me in the eyes and said "I'm about to go through another election, but if I get re-elected, you get out of the Army, and I'm still around you will always have a job here." I was shocked but pleasantly surprised because I didn't think that I had made an impression on the sheriff in such a short period of time. Isaac soon showed back up and he and I left together.

A couple of weeks after my father's surgery he was released from the hospital and had transitioned to a rehabilitation center. The rehab center was about three miles away from my parent's home, which made it very convenient for my mom to visit with him as much as she wanted to. His recovery was moving along slowly but his rehab was very intense and rigorous. I went to visit him one day when I knew that he had rehab. I wanted to catch him while he was rehabbing because I wanted to take the opportunity to encourage him. One of the physical therapists had told my mom that she did not know if my dad was giving a maximum effort in regards to his rehab. When I walked in my dad was sitting on the leg curl machine and had just finished doing a set of repetitions. As I stood at the door watching he looked tired and discouraged. I said, "Big Ike, what's going on man?" He smiled and said, "Nothing much, bubba." I stayed with him for the duration of his work out that day. I looked him in his eyes and said, "Daddy you have always been there to push me and encourage me, but today is my turn to return the favor. I'm not going to let you quit, and no matter how tough your rehab is you are going to hit this heart condition before it hits you." He smiled at me and said "You are right, bubba!"

Chelice and I wondered where the time had gone because before we knew it, it was time to take the journey back to Germany. My father was feeling better and was well on his way back to recovering. This really gave me a piece of mind, but I still had a major decision that I had to make regarding my future. It was a long plane ride back but it didn't seem that long to me because I was deep in thought on the entire trip all the way back to Europe. I really didn't like the helpless feeling of not being able to get to my father as quickly as I wanted to. I really hadn't even spoken with my wife about it, but it was a major concern for me. We made it back to Germany safely, but I was starting to think that this would be the last time that my family would be traveling back to my duty station in Germany.

HIT'EM BEFORE THEY HIT YOU

****

The time came for me to decide whether or not I was going to re-up for another four years in the Army or get out and move closer to family and start a new career in law enforcement. The conversation that I had with Sheriff Cribb really had left a positive impression on me as it related to a possible career in law enforcement. Working in Georgetown would only put me about an hour and fifteen minutes away from Charleston in the event that I needed to get to my parents. I thought to myself, "I am already physically fit so I wouldn't have any problems making it through the South Carolina Criminal Justice Academy." I really believed that it couldn't be any worse than basic training at Fort Jackson. Another thing that would play a major role in his decision was the fact that my wife's family was from Georgetown, and this would give us the support staff that we didn't have while we were stationed in Germany. I also thought about my father and how he always sacrificed to take care of his family. This was the first real decision that I would make that would affect all of my loved ones and I really wanted to get it right. I knew that my wife would follow me to the end of the earth, but I could also feel that she really missed her family back in South Carolina. The positives just kept mounting in my mind regarding getting out of the Army and moving back to South Carolina and the only negative seemed to be having to start all over again with a new career.

I finally talked everything over with my wife, and just

like I figured she said, "I will support you in anything that you decide to do, honey, because I know that you will always do what is best for our family." My wife was certain of this because she knew how I was raised and how my father instilled in me that at the end of the day for a man it's all about taking care of his family. I explained to her that I felt like I needed to be closer to my parents as they got older, especially with my father's health declining, and that I felt like I was being called into a career in law enforcement. It was strange for me because I grew up in the church and when there was always talk about someone being called it was for them being called into some type of ministry. Chelice understood and was extremely excited about starting the next chapter in our lives and she was proud of me for really trying to do what I thought was best for our family. The decision had been made.

****

In the summer of 1997 my family made it back to Georgetown, South Carolina. Both Chelice's and my families were ecstatic that we were back in the States. They were more excited about face time with the kids than they were about seeing me and Chelice. Both sets of grandparents could not wait to get their hands on their grandchildren. For Chelice and I it was a circus trying to shuffle the kids back and forth between family and friends, but it was good to have help with the kids as we transitioned and started to look for work in the civilian world. We had spent our first three years as a family growing together away from close family and friends and had grown independent of needing help

HIT'EM BEFORE THEY HIT YOU

from anyone. We sometimes had to catch ourselves when family members would ask if we needed help with the kids, because we had grown accustomed to doing everything as a family. Prior to us moving back to the States we did not go anywhere or do anything that we couldn't include our children in. We would have to learn how to relax a little bit and let the rest of the family get to know and enjoy our children.

9
Service Begins

Matthew 5:9 Blessed are the peacemakers: for they shall be called the children of God.

As our family was getting settled in and re-acclimated to living in the United States, I did exactly what Sheriff Cribb had told me to do. I traveled to the Georgetown County Sheriff's Office the following week and filled out a job application. I didn't ask to see the sheriff or even ask for my brother-in-law Isaac. I had grown to be a proud man and did not want to be shown any favoritism and did not want anyone to think that I was looking for a favor or any handouts. I often thought about something that my grandfather James Drye, Sr. told me once. My grandfather was a veteran of the United States Air Force, and he also retired from the Federal Aviation Administration. He told me once that he tried to live his life the way James Brown sung about in one of his songs: "I don't want nobody to give me nothing, open up the door I'll get it myself." I tried to live the same way and always wanted my hard work and work ethic to speak for me. My father always taught me to think for myself and not follow the crowd, so I was always very independent. I filled out the application that day and returned it to one of the front desk clerks working at the window at the time.

Three weeks elapsed and I hadn't heard anything from the sheriff's office regarding my application. I saw my brother-in-law Isaac in passing one day and we struck up a conversation. He wanted to know how my transition to the civilian world was going. "I told him that things were going fine, but they would be going even better if I could hear something back from the Sheriff's Office regarding my job application,"

Isaac was surprised. "When did you apply, and why didn't you tell me?" "I didn't really want to make any fuss about it I just wanted to get my application in."

Isaac explained to me that it was all well and fine, but I should have mentioned it to him because they get so many applications and sometimes some of them get lost in the shuffle. Isaac immediately called the office to check on the status of my application. The clerk Isaac spoke with told him that they could not find an application with the name Kelvin Waites associated with it. Isaac asked me to get in his car and ride down to the sheriff's office with him. When we arrived Isaac took me directly to Sheriff Cribb's office. The sheriff was in and Isaac and I sat down and explained to him what was going on. The sheriff asked me to fill out another application and to give it directly to him as soon as I finished filling it out. I filled it out and the sheriff assured me that I would hear something very soon from his office.

The following week I was called in for an interview. There were three gentlemen who sat on the interview panel; Chief Deputy Willie Ben Grate, Chief Detective Bob Medlin, and Captain David Carter. Between these three gentlemen there was at least seventy years of law enforcement experience sitting in front of me. I was actually comfortable in this type of environment because I had experienced going through promotional boards while in the Army. They interviewed me for about an hour, but to me it just seemed like an hour-long conversation. They immediately offered me a job after the interview and I started working the beginning of the next week. There were two major things that impressed the panel to the point that they knew that they wanted to hire me. The first thing was the fact that they did everything that they could to rattle me and make me nervous, but I stayed calm over the course of the entire interview. I did not say "um," did not stutter, wasn't jittery, and I spoke with conviction and confidence. This was an indicator to the panel that they could depend on me to be cool and calm during times of high stress and in tense situations. The second thing was the way that I answered the question when I was asked why I wanted to be a law enforcement officer.

"I want to be a law enforcement officer because I care about children, I love helping people, and I think that it's law enforcement's job to help make the community better." The Georgetown County Sheriff's Office had a philosophy that featured community-oriented policing, and it appeared that I would be a perfect fit for what they were trying to accomplish.

I was extremely excited about becoming a law

HIT'EM BEFORE THEY HIT YOU

enforcement officer, and wanted to be the best officer that I could possibly be. I was issued a weapon, a badge, my uniforms, and a patrol car. From the time that I was hired I had one month before I had to attend the South Carolina Criminal Justice Academy to obtain my law enforcement officer's certification. I, along with five of my peers, would spend that month being tutored and mentored by Captain David Carter, who was the training officer, for the Georgetown County Sheriff's Office. Captain Carter's job was to get the new hires who had to attend the academy ready by giving us some idea of the type of training we would be exposed to. Captain Carter was an older gentleman who appeared to be in his mid- to late-fifties. He was medium-sized, appeared to be about five feet, seven inches tall; he had gray receding hair, but he appeared to be in pretty good shape for his age. He tutored us on state laws and legal updates, fire arms training, as well as emergency vehicle operations. I did not have any problems with the training and I couldn't wait to go to the academy.

My mother was still trying to warm up to the idea of me becoming a police officer. She always worried and prayed for all three of her sons, but she couldn't understand why I would leave one dangerous career to walk right into another one. She would always say to me, "You know, Kelvin, there are some evil, wicked, and crazy people in this world and you really have to be careful." I would always smile at her and say, "Now momma, you are a God-fearing Christian woman and you know that God has everything under control and besides, I'm a lil' crazy, too." Even though she worried she knew that I had a special calling on my life and that I would be okay. She always felt like my calling consisted of me being a preacher and having my own church. I would often tell my mom that "I am called to the ministry of law enforcement, and the streets will be my pulpit." I thanked God every day that I had a wife and children who supported me in my career path. I knew how important it was for the family of a soldier or a law enforcement officer to support them. I saw so many times how the lack of support for service members or law enforcement officers led to the destruction of families. I learned that it takes a special family to support a law enforcement officer. It takes a special family to deal with the long hours and shift work. It takes a special family to understand why only mom can be at sporting events and school activities because daddy has to work. It takes a special family to understand Saturday mornings when the kids want daddy to watch cartoons, but he is just too tired because he just got off of night shift. I felt blessed to have such a wonderful support system as I started my new career.

I attended the Criminal Justice Academy in Columbia, South Carolina, for eight weeks. The Basic Law Enforcement Course reminded me of basic training for the U.S. Army a little bit. It was not as intense, but it focused more on the classroom activities than the Army basic training did. My roommate at the Criminal Justice Academy was a guy named Eric Watson. He was actually from my hometown of Charleston, South Carolina. Eric was brown-skinned, five feet, eleven inches tall and looked very athletic, like he was a football or rugby player. Eric was a real nice and soft-spoken guy. On the other hand I loved to play jokes on people and had a very good sense of humor. This mixture would prove to be the perfect balance to get us both through the academy. We would spend a lot of time working out and studying together, pushing each other to do as well as we could at the South Carolina Criminal Justice Academy. Eric advanced in his career and today is the major of public information for the Charleston County Sheriff's Office.

I, along with the rest of my classmates, was allowed to travel home on the weekends to get away from the academy for a couple of days. This made going through the eight-week training even easier, because I would go home every weekend, see my loved ones, and be reminded of why I wanted to become a law enforcement officer in the first place. It also made it seem as if the academy went by a lot faster. Every weekend that I would travel home it seemed like Jasmin and K.J. had grown so much. It did me good to see their little eyes light up as I walked in the door Friday evening after a two-and-a-half-hour drive home from the police academy. I would play with them Friday nights when I got home until they got tired. My wife and I would catch each other up on everything that was going on during our absence away from each other. She would tell me how work was going for her, and the wacky things that the kids would do over the course of the week. I would tell her funny stories and things that I experience at the Criminal Justice Academy. On Saturday mornings I would get up early and make the "Isaac Waites famous pancakes" just like my dad would do for my older brother and me. I had the opportunity to train with people who would become law enforcement professionals all over the state of South Carolina, and as the years passed I would bump into and cross paths with some of those same people.

In August of 1997 and I graduated from the South Carolina Criminal Justice Academy. I could not wait to get back to work so that I could start to learn everything that I could about Georgetown County.

When I reported to work for the first time I was assigned to Sgt. Matthew Grayson's shift. He was a Marine Corps veteran and that is how he carried himself all day, every day. He appeared to be in his mid-forties at the time. Sgt. Grayson was about five feet, eight inches tall, slim built, dark skinned, and in good shape. He was a God-fearing family man. When we first met he told me that he knew something was different about me. He assigned me to my training officer but wanted to sit down with me before I hit the streets. Sgt. Grayson told me three things that would define me as a person and define my law enforcement career: "Trust in God, don't get caught up with gossip and little groups around the office, and always try to do things to make the community better." I really respected Sgt. Grayson and for some reason, he reminded me of my father. I learned a lot from Sgt. Grayson and would sometimes visit his church to fellowship with him and his family. I was trained by a field training officer for about six weeks before I was cut loose to work on my own.

I really began to enjoy being a deputy sheriff and I knew I had made the right decision regarding my career path. Just like many other young law enforcement officers, my focus was to catch the bad guy and put him in jail. At that point in my career I had no idea that there was so much more to being a law enforcement officer.

HIT'EM BEFORE THEY HIT YOU

As a patrol officer I saw so many different things on a daily basis.

I would encounter people who wanted to kill themselves, bank robbers, drug dealers, rapist, mental patients; I found myself in just about every situation that you could think of. I seemed to thrive under pressure and did not shy away from taking any type of call. I always had a knack for dealing with people and bringing a certain level of calmness to just about any situation I was involved in. I really had a way about me that caused people to cling to me, even if I had to take them to jail. I had compassion for people and would always say to myself, "He may be a drug dealer or some other type of criminal, but he is still somebody's child." As a result of that I would always get tips and information from the community that some other officers wouldn't be privy to. I was slow to anger and would only increase my intensity if I had to. I would see guys in the street I had arrested and they would come up to me and speak without any hatred or malice in their hearts. I routinely patrolled the roughest parts of the county, and would get out on the street corner and talk to young men if I saw them hanging around. This sometimes led to good dialogue between me and the young men of the community, but it sometimes led to a foot chase that resulted in someone going to jail for possession of drugs or being a wanted person.

I was in tune with what was going on in the communities throughout Georgetown County, and my incident report writing skills would provide me with other job opportunities within the Georgetown County Sheriff's Office. I eventually got the opportunity to work as a narcotics investigator, as well as a criminal investigator. I even got an opportunity to work as an investigator for the Solicitor's/District Attorney's Office. There was one thing that continued to bother me, though. I had been in law enforcement for about eight years now, which was long enough to cycle through arresting fathers of families and then having to arrest their sons. The cycle of criminal activity within families bothered me because I had a big heart when it came to the young people. I saw the youth as the future and really wanted to do my part to help them. I wanted to come up with ideas for the sheriff's office to be more proactive in trying to get the youth in the community to focus on positive things instead of being pulled toward negative things. When I served as lieutenant of the narcotics unit at the sheriff's office, I requested to have a meeting with my assistant sheriff to discuss something. When I met with him, I said, "I feel like something is missing and I don't think that we are doing enough to help the community." It didn't seem that the assistant sheriff really understood what I was telling him.

"You arrest bad people, you are a good husband, and a good father; what more do you want?" he asked. I agreed with what he said, but I told him that I still didn't think that we were doing enough to have a positive impact on the children in the community. That meeting ended with me being determined for the Sheriff's Office to get more involved with the young people of Georgetown County, even though I didn't know where to start.

For about two months after I met with Assistant Sheriff Weaver, I beat myself up and wracked my brain on what we needed to be doing. One day I got an

HIT'EM BEFORE THEY HIT YOU

unexpected phone call. I was in my office one afternoon when a call was transferred to me. I answered the phone and heard a female voice say, "Yes, my name is Genola Williams, and I am with the Murrells Inlet Elks Lodge."

"Yes ma'am, this is Lieutenant Waites; how can I help you"?

Mrs. Williams wanted to know from me what the Georgetown County Sheriff's Office was doing to help educate young people in the community about the negative effects of drugs. She was not happy with the answer I gave her. I told Mrs. Williams that my unit conducted long- and short-term narcotic investigations and did the best that we could to take illegal and dangerous drugs off of the streets. Mrs. Williams thought that I was trying to elude her question, but I really didn't have a legitimate answer for her. She decided to invite me to lunch the following week at the Murrells Inlet Elks Lodge. I arrived at the Elks Lodge at 11:50 a.m. to meet with Mrs. Williams. When I reached the door I told the attendant who I was meeting for lunch and the attendant walked me over to a table where an elderly woman was sitting. She appeared to be in her late sixties. She was short, had red hair, and I could tell that she was a very proud and distinguished lady. "I am so glad that you took the time to come and meet with me today," she said. She spoke with elegance and conviction to me that day regarding educating young people about the negative effects of drugs. I could tell that she really had a passion for serving children. This would be the first of many meetings between Mrs. Williams and I. That day she made me aware of the fact that National Red Ribbon week was approaching, which was a national

89

drug prevention campaign. As Mrs. Williams and I continued to meet our planning committee grew more and more. We all had come up with the idea of having a Kids' Festival and Red Ribbon Parade on Front Street in Georgetown that would conclude at East Bay Park, which is located right in the middle of Winyah Bay. Our committee planned multiple activities for the children of the community at East Bay Park. We planned to feed the children with food, fun, and education. We discussed having face painting, bounce houses, motivational speakers, and several other activities for the children. As the word spread throughout the community, more and more organizations and stakeholders stepped up to the plate and wanted to help and be a part of the event. The event was fully sponsored, all of the food and services were donated, and the children and their families did not have to pay for anything. All they had to do was show up. The steering committee worked hard to advertise the event on television, the radio, as well as the newspapers.

On the day of the event I was extremely excited as well as nervous about the possible turnout for the event. On that day it came full circle for me and I realized that this was what I had talking to Assistant Sheriff Weaver about the day I told him that I didn't think that we were doing enough. I hoped and prayed for a large turnout. The committee had planned an awesome day for the kids and had prepared to feed about three thousand children and their families. It started off with the Red Ribbon Parade. The steering committee had invited all local organizations, high school bands, and any children who wanted to participate in the parade. The parade was a hit and the turnout of onlookers watching the parade

HIT'EM BEFORE THEY HIT YOU

was a sight to see. From the beginning of the parade you could tell that the community had really showed up to support its young people and you could just feel the energy. The parade rolled right into the Kids' Festival. There were kids everywhere having fun, eating, and getting educated about the negative effects of drugs. The steering committee estimated that they served about thirty-two hundred children on that day. The committee was able to get Robert Geathers, Jr., who played for the Cincinnati Bengals at the time, to come that day and speak to the children about doing the right things. Robert was someone the children could actually relate to because he was born and raised in Georgetown, South Carolina, and went on to play in the NFL.

At one point I saw Mrs. Williams standing off in the distance all alone. I decided to walk over to see if she was okay. Mrs. Williams hugged me and started crying and all she kept saying was, "I'm just so happy." As I hugged Mrs. Williams my eyes filled up with tears because I had just figured out what true service was all about. I finally experienced that being a law enforcement officer was more than just writing tickets, kicking in doors, and arresting people. I had a feeling on the inside that I had never felt before. I was happy deep down in my soul that I had done a small part in making something positive happen for the children of my community. I also remembered what my father told me about the three things that I needed to do to be successful in life. Up until the point that I met Mrs. Williams I had been trusting in God and working hard. The thing that was missing was going out of my way to do something to help someone else. That is why I felt so uneasy and

91

unfulfilled up until that point. I now understood why my father cried in Harlem that Sunday morning while sitting at the table with my older brother and me. There were no other words that could possibly come to mind other than, I was just happy. Watching all of the hard work that our steering committee put into making a positive impact on the children in our community really touched me. Watching it all fall in place was overwhelming. At that moment I knew exactly how my father felt.

The event that we founded turned into an annual event that takes place at East Bay Park the Saturday before Mother's Day every year. I now understood what service was all about.

HIT'EM BEFORE THEY HIT YOU

10
The Conference

Proverbs 1:5 A wise man will hear, and will increase learning; and a man of understanding shall attain unto wise counsel.

One morning, during the summer of 2004, I met three friends for breakfast. I would meet the same group of young men once a week at a little breakfast shop in Pawleys Island. We would talk about current events, sports, personal issues, or sometimes just meet to read a scripture and have fellowship. I loved to fellowship with Van, Horace, and Noel. Van was a pastor at a local church in the area and he had a big heart when it came to children. He was a graduate of Clemson University and was a member of their National Championship football team in 1982. He was a very humble man. Horace, on the other hand, was a loud but a real funny guy. He was a Christian who really found God after living in the fast lane for a period of time. Horace loved to cook and sell food, but he would do any type of handy work that he could to help someone in the community or make an honest living. The guys used to call Horace "Spoon" because he was always trying to stir something up, but everyone knew that he had a heart of gold. Noel was a local police officer. He was always steady, and was a very talented musician. He could sing and play the piano like an angel. When the four of us got together we would have some serious conversations, most times facilitated by Van.

Toward the end of our meeting on this particular day, Van looked at me and said, "Hey man, Horace, Noel, and I are going to a conference in Dallas in a couple of weeks; would you like to go?" I was shocked and surprised by the random question because we had just spent the past hour talking, eating, laughing, and nobody mentioned anything about a conference. Van could tell that I was in deep thought and my hesitation caused Van to say, "You don't have to tell me right now." He told me to just think about it, talk to my wife, and let him know in about a week or so. Van assured me that my plane ticket, hotel room, and registration for the conference would all be taken care of and that I would only need to bring money for meals. This was almost too good to be true for me, because I am a lifelong Dallas Cowboys fan and would love to see their stadium, if given the opportunity. I left this meeting surprised and really didn't know how to take the invitation. I was always skeptical of anyone who tried to go out of their way to do anything nice for me. Because I was in law enforcement, I didn't want anyone doing something nice for me and expecting to be paid back for it later with some type of favor. I couldn't help but think, "Free plane ticket to Dallas, free hotel, free registration to a conference, there has to be an angle." I inquired about how long the conference was and what type of conference it was. Van told me that the conference lasted one week and it was a leadership conference at Bishop T.D. Jakes' church.

I called my wife when I was on his way home and told her that she was not going to believe what I had to tell her when I got home. Just like anyone else she was a little nervous about what I had to say and did not want to wait until I got home. I didn't budge and I made Chelice wait until I got home before I told her what was going on. Of course when I walked in the door she gave me the look like, "Okay, give it up." I told her about the trip, but also told her that I was not really sure if I wanted to go. I had reservations because my mother-in-law was fighting cancer at the time and I just thought that it was a bad time to leave. I was also skeptical of Van's motives for inviting me. After I told Chelice about the trip I was very surprised by her response. She said, "You work hard, you never go anywhere, and you need to take this opportunity to get away and relax." I didn't say anything, but I knew that she was right and I knew that everything happened for a reason.

The following week I called Pastor Van to let him know that I had thought about it and had decided that I was going to take him up on his offer. Van was ecstatic and appeared to be more excited about me going than I was. About a week later it was time to fly to Dallas and all of us met at the Myrtle Beach International Airport. The travel agenda was for us to fly to San Antonio and then on to Dallas. We had a nice comfortable flight and made it safely to Dallas. We rented a car at the airport and drove straight to the Marriot in downtown Dallas. After we got settled in at the hotel we rode over to the Potter's

House, which is Bishop T.D. Jakes' church, to register for the conference and pick up our packets. When we got close enough to see the Potter's House we were all amazed at the facility and the amount of cars parked in the parking lot. I noticed how they had several security officers in the area getting people situated in the parking lot and safely across the street. I could not believe what I saw and would have never imagined that a church could be so big and beautiful. I thought to myself, "If I didn't know any better I would think that I was pulling up to an NBA basketball arena to attend a professional basketball game." We went in and registered and got our packets and identification cards. We walked into the book store that was right inside of the doorway of the church. It was about the size of a Barnes & Nobles filled with CDs, books, and other inspirational publications. I thought to myself while I stood in the middle of that book store that someday I would have a book on these same shelves. From the time Pastor Van asked me to go on the trip, on the plane ride over, on the way to the hotel, and on the drive over to the conference there was a question that I just couldn't answer.

It was really driving me crazy because I could not figure out why I was invited to attend the conference. As time went on it appeared to me that the conference was geared toward parishioners, pastors, and those who were active in some type of ministry. The three gentlemen that I traveled with were all in some type of ministry. Van was a pastor who had his own local church called "The Father's House." Noel was the minister of music at Van's church, and was actively taking classes in pursuit of a degree in theology. Horace was a deacon in Van's church. Horace also mentored the young men of the church and encouraged them to not make some of the same mistakes that he did. I thought to myself, "I'm just a lieutenant in charge of the narcotics division at the Georgetown County Sheriff's Office and I'm not a part of any type of ministry." It just didn't make sense to me; I knew that there was a reason that I was there, but I just didn't know what that reason was yet.

I had the opportunity over the course of the week to listen to some dynamic and powerful speakers. It was an awesome experience and before I knew it I was having the time of my life. We heard speakers such as T.D. Jakes and Juanita Bynum. We also heard some of the best gospel artists in the world perform. The theme of the conference was "Lead While You Bleed." Every speaker touched on the fact that if you were called into the ministry or if you were chosen to lead people, it was only because God chose you to do so. They all made sure that everyone understood that it wasn't just about being called to a ministry, but everyday leaders are also chosen by God to lead. As I was listening to Bishop Jakes speak toward the end of the conference it all became clear to me. I realized that the conference was not just geared toward just parishioners, pastors, and leaders within their ministries. Instead, this conference was about being a leader in general in whatever field that you were in. The entire message on leadership and the purpose that I was invited to the conference was revealed to me. The conference changed me and the type of leader that I was for the rest of my life.

What I learned during the conference was that "you lead while you bleed" is all about sacrifice and not only carrying my load as a leader, but in some cases carrying the load of the people that you are called to lead. I realized that as a leader I was not exempt from issues in my personal life, but I realized that as a leader I had to put my garbage aside, stay focused, and continue to lead my people. In terms of leadership I realized that this is what separated the men and women from the boys and the girls, because everyone who calls themselves a leader cannot pull it off. You and your spouse may not be getting along, your kids may be acting out, or you may not feel good, but in the eyes of your people "you cannot afford to have a bad day because you set the tone." Just because you are beat up emotionally and may be bleeding on the inside, you cannot let it spill over and affect the morale of your people. When you are responsible for leading people it cannot just be about X's and O's or just being task- or result-driven. I also learned that if you are truly called to lead people, it may be tough, but a true leader sets aside his own well-being to take care of his people. In essence, "you lead while you bleed."

This conference helped me understand what my father experienced as a leader over the course of his entire life. If anyone was able to lead while they bled, it was Isaac Waites. I thought to myself, "I came all the way to Dallas to learn how to really serve and lead people." I realized that sometimes God has to get you out of your comfort zone and away from every distraction in your life in order to deal with you. We had a great time at the conference and each of us walked away with something different to put in our hearts and minds. We would never forget our trip to Dallas. The crazy

HIT'EM BEFORE THEY HIT YOU

thing is that I had such a great and powerful time at the conference, that I forgot all about going to see the Dallas Cowboys football stadium. The Lord really does work in mysterious ways. He allowed me to travel to Dallas thinking that it was for one reason, knowing that he had a whole different purpose for me being there. I could not thank Pastor Van enough for letting God use him to get me to the conference, because it truly changed my life. Nobody I worked with knew where I was at for the week that I was gone. Everyone just thought that I had finally decided to take some time off and just hang out with my family, because I never took any time off. They had no idea of the transformation that I went through.

Before leaving for the conference I was the type of supervisor that was results-driven. I pushed my people to their limits on a daily basis, and demanded their best at all times. I never really took the time to really get to know the people who worked with me and for me. All I cared about was getting the job done. I now knew that I needed to really get to know my people. I wanted to know what really made them tick, and be more compassionate to their needs. I made it my first order of business to sit down with each and every one of my subordinates after the conference. I talked with them about their families, their goals, encouraged them to continue their education, and made it clear to them that they could call on me twenty-four hours a day, and seven days a week if they needed me. I learned their children's names, their birthdates, and their wedding anniversaries. Prior to the conference it was only a one-sided relationship between us, where I demanded maximum output from them. It was now time for me to even the scale out and equally give back to them. What did I have to offer? I offered them the support they needed to do their jobs and take care of their families. I offered them the same compassion that I expected them to have for the public and citizens we served. I offered them someone who would carry their load for them a little while whenever they got too tired to carry it. I truly adopted a theory of "I cannot afford to have a bad day" in spite of what may or may not be going on in my personal life. I realized that I had people who depended on me and I had to be totally open and accessible to them. I was reminded of something that my father learned as a child. I learned that "charity also begins at home," even in the work place. How could I possibly expect my people to go out and serve the community when I was not serving them? I made sure that my people understood that it was very important for them to take care of their families, because family really does come first. As a leader there is no way that I can count on my subordinates to come to work and be productive if their family lives are falling apart at home. I continued to go on in my career mentoring many supervisors and discussing the theory of "you lead while you bleed" with them.

11
What can I say?

Philippians 4:13 "I can do all things through Christ which strengthens me."

It was about 12:55 a.m. in the morning on April 27, 2009, when my mom called me. I am an extremely light sleeper so I actually answered the phone right after the first ring. I was used to getting calls from my officers late at night when major things happened so it wasn't that unusual for my phone to be ringing at that time of night. I did not get a chance to view the caller I.D. before I answered, but when I heard the soft voice of my mother I knew that this was not a good call. My mother never called me this late unless something very serious was going on. I braced myself for what might come next, expecting the worse. After I said hello my mother calmly said, "Well Kelvin, Isaac is gone." I immediately felt like I had all of the air knocked out of my body. I asked her what happened and she told me that he just passed away in his sleep. I told my mom that I was on the way to Charleston and that I would see her shortly. She asked me to call Bryan and Terrance to let them know what had happened. I can remember riding in the car and saying to myself, "Lord if I am going to have a moment and cry please let me go ahead and get it out of the way on the car ride down to Charleston." I knew that I was going to have to be strong for my mom and the rest of my family, which would be a very hard thing to do. As bad as I wanted to cry, I couldn't because I just felt numb.

On the ride down I thought about an episode that my father had about thirty days prior to him passing away. He had become very sick and had been hospitalized at Roper Hospital in downtown Charleston. His blood pressure had continued to drop slowly while his organs had started to shut down. During that episode it had reached a point that he was put on a ventilator because he was not breathing on his own. I can remember standing beside his bed in the Intensive Care Unit and whispering under my breath "that's not my dad; he has already gone to heaven." His skin color had already changed and it was obvious to me that the only thing that was keeping him with us was that ventilator that was breathing for him. It looked like all of the life had seeped out of his body. On that particular day I went home with a heavy heart, thinking that it was only a matter of time before my daddy was gone. The following day I went back to the hospital to check on my dad, and as I walked through the door leading into the Intensive Care Unit I heard what sounded like my father's voice. I said to myself as I walked down the short hallway "that can't be him talking." As I reached his room I saw a nurse standing over his bed, and I heard my dad tell the nurse "ma'am please just leave me alone; I'm tired." The nurse immediately looked at me and said, "Sir, are you his son"? I answered her yes and asked her what was going on. She told me that miraculously my dad's blood pressure had increased this morning and he started to breathe on his own. She went on to tell me, "the only problem now is that he needs a dialysis treatment and he is refusing it." The nurse then told me that if my father did not get that treatment he would die. I asked the nurse to give my dad and me some privacy so that we could talk for a minute and she left the room. I said to my dad, "Now Ike, you know that you have to get this dialysis treatment unless you are going to die." My father sat up slightly in his hospital bed, looked me directly in my eyes, and said, "Kelvin it's okay; I have already talked with God." I told him in a joking way that I understood his conversation with God but he was going to have to take the dialysis treatment on that day. I always had a way with my dad, and I was able to convince him to take his dialysis treatment that day. My father recovered from his episode and was released from the hospital a couple of days later. I joked about it but I really believed that the day before when he was not breathing and the life was slowly draining out of his body that he did talk with God. I believe that even though he did speak with God it wasn't quite his time and God told him, "Not yet, Isaac."

On the ride down to my mom's house it all became clear and made sense to me. God didn't take my dad away thirty days prior because he wanted to give the family time to get ourselves prepared and get our act together.

When I made it to Charleston, the funeral home had already transported my father's body to their facility. My mom and I just sat around talking, making phone calls, still in shock all at the same time. For me it did not even seem real and I did not want to accept the fact that a part of me was gone.

A few days passed and my brothers and the rest of my family started to arrive and congregate in Charleston for my father's home-going service. My Uncle Stevie came from San Antonio. My Aunt Lizzie traveled to Charleston from New York City. My Aunt Deloris flew in from Boston, Massachusetts. People were coming from all over the country to pay respects to my dad. Just like with any other family it was great seeing family I hadn't seen in years, but I just wish it wasn't under those circumstances. It was amazing to see all of the family come together and all of the people who stopped by just to pay their respects to the family. It was obvious that Isaac Waites had touched many lives in a positive way, and that fact alone comforted me as I dealt with his passing.

The day had come for my mom, my brothers, and I to go to the funeral home to make all of the arrangements for my father's funeral. We decided the color of the casket, the clothing that he would wear, and the seating arrangements inside of the limousines. We started working on the actual order of the service. We talked about things such as his favorite songs and hymns, as well as who would give his eulogy. Then something happened that I was not prepared for. My mother asked me to speak about my father at his home-going service on behalf of the family. My first thoughts and emotions were, "There is no way that I can do it." I just looked at my mom, nodded my head, and said okay. I remember thinking selfishly to myself, "I really don't want to do this." Even though that I realized that we all had to leave here at some point, I never in a million years thought that I would be asked to speak over my father at his funeral. Of course after my mother asked me to do it I pretty much zoned out and really didn't hear what was going on during the rest of the meeting at the funeral home. As I sat quietly at the table in the conference room of the funeral home, a soft voice whispered in my ear, "What's your problem; that's the least that you can do." It was sobering to hear that voice and the truth of the matter was it was true. I should have been proud and honored at the fact that my mom asked me to speak over my dad. Speaking at my dad's funeral was small in comparison to everything that he had done for me. I kept thinking to myself, "There is so much; what can I say?" We finalized the arrangements for my father's wake and funeral at the funeral home that evening then we all went back to my mother's house to continue to meet and greet family and friends.

The days seemed to be slipping by very quickly and the funeral was quickly approaching. I had stayed very busy picking family up from the airport and train station, making sure the garbage was dumped at my mother's home, and making sure that there was enough ice. I paused for a minute and realized that even though days had passed I had still had not shed a tear. I had been on the verge a couple of times but it just did not happen. It was actually starting to feel like I was carrying a one hundred-pound rucksack on my back. For some reason I just couldn't squeeze it out. My fear was that I would finally break down when I got up to speak, and that would not be the appropriate time, because I really wanted to do my dad justice.

The visitation went off without any problems and finally it was the day of the funeral. Time just seemed to have flown by so fast. I could tell that everything was starting to wear my mother down and I could not wait for this day to be over. Bryan, Terrance, and I did our best to stick close to my mom because we knew that she was having an extremely tough time with everything. Before we all realized it the limousines had pulled up in front of my mother's house and were just about ready to escort the family downtown to Nichols Chapel AME Church for my dad's funeral service. The ride was normally about a 15-minute ride but on this particular day it felt like the ride was about two hours long. The closer we got to the church the more I thought about the task I had to complete. On the way to the funeral in the limousine I jotted a couple of notes down on a piece of paper.

We arrived at the church and were escorted into the church. I can remember saying to myself, "This is the hardest thing up until this point in my life that I ever had to do." The family marched in past my dad's casket and the family was all seated. The church was packed with family and friends. I really don't recall much of the service because all I could focus on was what I was going to say. As I sat in my seat my mind start moving in one hundred different directions. I found myself daydreaming about things that I had learned from my father during our time together. I thought about how he taught me that I can do anything in life that I wanted

HIT'EM BEFORE THEY HIT YOU

to do. "Reach for the sky; the sky is the limit" is what he would often tell us. He taught me that it was okay to be different, and to be my own man. He would say, "Kelvin, think for yourself; you don't just have to go along with the crowd." He taught me that no matter what I go through during my life it is my job to make sure that I push my children to do better. It didn't matter that he had limited education as well as resources because he knew that he was responsible for making sure that we had more than he did and reach our full potential. I thought about how he taught me that nobody would give me anything, and how I would have to fight to achieve my goals. My dad taught me that my dreams are like stars, and if I let go I will surely fall. He taught me to always be respectful and humble no matter what my status in life may be. He showed me how to be a good leader as well as a good father. He did this by showing up, encouraging us, and not just telling us, but showing us. He was always positive despite how bad the situation may have seemed. He taught me that if I wanted to be successful in life I had to trust in God, work hard, and to always do something to help others. I remember sitting there during the service and thinking, "I don't even know where to begin."

The time had come for me to speak and both Bryan and Terrance accompanied me up to the pulpit area. I acknowledged my mom and the rest of the family and then I said, "What can I say?" I went on to tell the congregation, "He taught my brothers and I how to be men and take care of our families." I made sure everyone knew that he didn't teach us by telling us, but he taught us by the example he set every day. I told everyone, "No matter what was going on in my life he was always there to encourage me." My dad taught me to never give up or quit, and even if you get off track just dust yourself off and get right back in the fight. I shared with everyone how my father stood with me at the football field of life and told me to "Hit 'em before they hit you." I could have talked all day about the many lessons and things that my father had taught me, but that was not the proper platform to do it. That is why I wrote this book. I wrote this book with the hope that something in between these covers will inspire someone to keep on pushing. I wrote this book with the hope that some father would be encouraged to be there for his kids. I wrote this book so that leaders would understand the sacrifice needed to push their people and their teams to the next level. I wrote this book because I truly believe that the world needs to hear the story of Isaac Waites and how he positively impacted everyone around him. I was so relieved after I said my piece about my dad and sat back down in my seat.

After most of my family from out of town had all traveled back to their respective places, things slowed down tremendously for my family. I decided that I would take a couple of days off at the start of the week because I had not really had any time for myself to process everything. I was at home alone and decided to put something on the grill for Chelice and the kids. While I was grilling it started to rain lightly. I could smell the rain prior to the first drop falling to the ground. My dad loved the smell of rain, and at that moment I imagined him saying, "You smell that rain, bubba?" At that moment I finally broke down and cried for about ten minutes. As I wept I felt better and could feel a weight being lifted up off of me.

Epilogue

So now you have it all. You now know how a man from Johns Island, South Carolina, with a sixth-grade education managed to inspire, motivate, and mold me into who I am today. Who is Kelvin Waites? I am the son of the late Isaac Waites, Sr. and Frances Waites. I am the brother of Isaac Waites, Jr. and Terrance Waites. I am the husband of Chelice Waites, and the father of Jasmin and Kelvin Waites, Jr. I am the kid who had to wear braces on my legs as a small child because my legs were crooked. I am the kid who suffered from violent asthma attacks as a child that could be triggered by the slightest amount of dust. I am the little kid who had to endure and overcome bullying. I am the kid who once had a very low self-esteem. I am a graduate of Charleston Southern University with a bachelor's of science degree in organizational management. I am a graduate of the prestigious F.B.I. National Academy (Session #248), which is located in Quantico, Virginia. I am the Deputy Chief of Police at a law enforcement agency in one of the largest counties in the state of South Carolina. I am a friend and a mentor to some. I am a leader.

Make no mistake about it, I would not be who I am today if it had not been for the motivation, teachings, and sacrifices that my father Isaac Waites, Sr. made for our family. He always carried the torch for the Waites family. He always told us that our job was to keep things progressing and moving the family's legacy along. He said, "Don't do what me and your mom did, do better." He told us as children that when we had children we need to require them to do more than their parents did.

My father left a lasting impression of his legacy with me as well as my brothers because he did three specific things. He showed up, he encouraged us, and he just didn't tell us but he showed us. He showed up to support me no matter what was going on. If it was football practice or a football game, he showed up. If it was a basketball game or a track meet, he showed up. If I was involved in a program at the church, he showed up. If I wasn't doing what I was supposed to do in school or anyplace else, he showed up. My dad didn't let the fact that he lost his childhood at an early age because he had to support his family stop him from showing up for his kids. He didn't let the fact that life may have dealt him a hand of cards that nobody would envy cause him to take his children's dreams for granted. He always encouraged us to do our very best. He encouraged me when times were good and not so good. He always told us to reach for the sky because the sky was the limit. He told me not to let anyone tell me what I could not do. My father told me that if anyone ever told me that I couldn't do something to turn that negative energy around and use it to show the world that I could. He encouraged us to step out from the crowd, be independent, think for ourselves, and be leaders. My father encouraged us to do those things knowing that sometimes we would have to stand alone for what we believed in or what we thought was right. He didn't just tell me how to be a man, he showed me. He showed me by the manner that he provided and took care of his family. He showed me how to be a leader by always being calm no matter what was going on, even when things seemed to be pretty bad.

HIT 'EM BEFORE THEY HIT YOU

He showed me how to be a man by sacrificing for the well-being of his loved ones and everyone else around him. He showed me how to be a leader by stepping up to the plate and making tough decisions that had a direct impact on everyone around him. He showed us how to be leaders by never ever complaining about life's ups and downs, knowing that God had everything in control.

That day at the football field when my dad told me to "hit 'em before they hit you," he set me free from everything negative that had happened in my life up to that particular point. I came out of my shell that day and for the first time in my life I felt good about myself and realized that I was good enough. Good enough to do anything that I wanted to do and good enough to be anything that I wanted to be. As a kid playing football for the first time in my life my dad gave me the very best advice that he could at the time, but it was about so much more than football. I just didn't apply my father's advice to football, but I took it with me throughout my life. As I interact with my children and my family today I strive to be just like my dad, knowing that if I end up being half the man that he was then everything will be okay.

He also had a very powerful impact on my career in the military as well as law enforcement. The fortitude that he displayed over the course of his life was the same fortitude that helped me to make it through basic training as well as one of the toughest technical schools in the U.S. Army. As a patrol officer, I had compassion for people and the community because of how I was raised by my father. As an undercover narcotics investigator I was able to stay calm in very dangerous situations, because I never saw my father panic in any situation. As a supervisor, I am able to put my people first because of the way that I saw my father lead his family, putting his own personal well-being on the back burner. My father is the reason I have always strived to be the best that I could be during my law enforcement career. He is the sole reason that I have had the drive and desire to train with law enforcement leaders from around the world on two different occasions. I had the opportunity to train at Quantico at the Drug Enforcement Administration's Academy (session #60) for two weeks, and then the FBI National Academy (session #248) for ten weeks. These two schools are the highlights of my career and I do not take for granted that most law enforcement officers never make it to those schools. I attribute my selection to those schools to the seeds of perseverance and excellence that my father planted in me, as you attend these prestigious schools by invitation only.

I remembered one day during the Christmas holiday before he passed away, my father telling me, "Kelvin, I have done my job. I raised you guys, took care of ya'll, and made sure that you all became productive citizens. I thank God for allowing me to live long enough to see it and even meet my grandchildren during the process. I consider myself blessed and I thank God for waking me up every day. I've done my part, son. I have lived my life and at this point everything else is gravy." He told me that he did not have any regrets and that he wouldn't change a thing about his life. This all came from a man whose health had declined over the years to the point that he could not take care of himself any longer. Nobody ever heard him complain. On April 27, 2009,

HIT'EM BEFORE THEY HIT YOU

my father was called home. It was so ironic to me that on his obituary there was a section that was titled "My Life was A Blessed Life." That section is mentioned below.

"My Life was A Blessed Life"

"When I was born the plan was written for me. I just lived the plan with God's help each day. I have fought a good fight, I have finished my course, and I have kept the faith."

This really took me back and reminded me of that Christmas when he said to me, "at this point everything else is gravy." When I read that passage on my father's obituary I knew without a shadow of doubt that it was all good and that everything would be okay. I often tell my children about their grandfather and all of the great things that he had done. I also tell them about the sacrifices that he made for our family and his teachings. I tell my children today to "hit 'em before they hit you" and go out and get it because nobody will give it to you. I know that my father's legacy still lives. My confirmation of this was one day when my sixteen-year-old son sent me a text message that said, "If you don't hunt, you don't eat." I sighed and could not help thinking, "that sounds like something my dad would say."

KELVIN WAITES

CPSIA information can be obtained at www.ICGtesting.com
Printed in the USA
BVOW08s1705150816

459036BV00001B/1/P